The
ALAMO CITY
GUIDE

The ALAMO CITY

GUIDE

Best attractions, dining, nightlife,
accommodations, and fun
in San Antonio

PARIS PERMENTER & JOHN BIGLEY

TWO LANE PRESS, INC.

Other books by Paris Permenter and John Bigley:
Day Trips From San Antonio and Austin (2nd ed.)
Texas Barbecue

First printing May 1995

ISBN: 1-878686-15-1

Printed in the United States of America

Cover and text design: Jim Langford
Cover photo: Paris Permenter and John Bigley
Editing: Jane Doyle Guthrie

10 9 8 7 6 5 4 3 2 1   95 96 97 98 99

Two Lane Press, Inc.
4245 Walnut Street
Kansas City, Missouri 64111

CONTENTS

ACKNOWLEDGMENTS

To write about San Antonio, we sought the advice of two groups: long time San Antonians and San Antonio travelers. From both groups, we learned to love the city even more, and to both groups we say *muchas gracias.*

We began our historic research at the San Antonio Conservation Society library. We thank the librarians and volunteers there who helped us search through newspaper clippings, scrapbooks, and historic documents that traced the evolution of the city's top attractions.

From there, we relied on the San Antonio Convention and Visitors Bureau where folks like Ernie Loeffler, Anna Buehrer, and Sharon Garcia kept us up-to-date on the Alamo City's newest hot spots.

Next, we made our way throughout the city, talking to shopkeepers, restaurateurs, and hoteliers about their establishments.

We took the advice of vacationers, visitors who, as the saying goes, just want to have fun. We brought our own amusement ride testers, Liz and Lauren Bigley, to the theme parks to give us their opinions on stomach-churners we didn't dare board. We talked to folks who came to San Antonio as visitors, ones who had made their first visit to HemisFair nearly three decades before and others who were being introduced to the city for the first time.

Finally, we depended on the people who, on a day-to-day basis, make San Antonio tourism work: the residents themselves. They share their city with an enthusiasm and friendliness that's rare these days. To all the museum docents, the bus drivers, the waiters, the ticket takers, and the tour guides, we give our thanks.

SAN ANTONIO

INTRODUCTION

Bienvenidos to the Alamo City! You've chosen a destination that combines the best of Texas, the Southwest, and Mexico into a city that's filled with fun and festivities.

Texans, whether residents of Amarillo or Zapata, have adopted San Antonio as their second hometown. When Texans think of a vacation spot in the Lone Star State, we look to the Alamo City. It brings back memories of childhood field trips to the Alamo, romantic strolls on the River Walk, Christmases beneath thousands of tiny lights, and family fun at the theme parks.

San Antonio is the number one tourist destination in the state according to the Texas Department of Transportation. The city's number of visitors is balanced by a population hovering at one million, ranking as the 10th largest city in the nation. But the numbers belie the real spirit of San Antonio. It's not just the number of attractions that draw visitors to this South Texas community; it's the atmosphere.

Will Rogers once proclaimed San Antonio "one of America's four unique cities." Wake up in the Alamo City with the scent of *huevos rancheros* in the air, the sound of mariachis filling the streets, and the sight of barges winding down the San Antonio River, and you'll know you're not in Kansas anymore, Dorothy. Even other Texas cities don't hold San Antonio's unique spirit.

Along with a strong Hispanic influence, San Antonio brings together other cultures to combine them into a unique flavor all its own. The German influence, begun during the city's early days, has left its mark on everything from architecture to menus. Old families that trace their heritage back to the days of the earliest San Antonio merchants have proudly worked to conserve the history of this city and to preserve its buildings and historic sites.

While other cities may speed along in the fast lane, San Antonio prefers the scenic route, a perfect pace for the city's many tourists who visit from around the world. Even though there are plenty of things to do, this is the kind of town where either a *siesta* or a museum is equally acceptable.

At the heart of the city is the San Antonio River, winding through tropical lushness and drawing residents and visitors into its current of gaiety along the riverbanks. The San Antonio River is to this city what the Seine is to Paris, the bay to San Francisco, the delta to New Orleans. It draws both residents and vacationers to its banks to enjoy a sense of place that is unrivaled anywhere else in Texas—and few places around the globe.

An old Spanish legend says, "They who drink of the San Antonio River will return." Drink up the atmosphere, soak up the sun that filters through the cypress and banana trees, and taste the excitement. And you'll be back.

A BIRD'S-EYE VIEW

San Antonio is a sprawling city, spanning 341 square miles that range from a dense downtown area to quiet suburban neighborhoods. The city is encircled by two loops: Loop 1604 traces the outside perimeter of the city, a boundary between the city and the untamed Hill Country where white-tailed deer still roam. Loop 410 (or I-410) lassoes the prime development in town, passing the San Antonio International Airport and skirting near all of the city's military bases.

San Antonio's spaghetti bowl of highways can seem daunting, so take a deep breath. Within the city, interstate highways divide the metropolis into several areas. I-35 runs an S-shaped curve through the city from northeast to southwest, skirting the downtown. I-10 runs northwest to downtown before taking an easterly turn. And I-37 defines the eastern boundary of downtown. To further confuse drivers, I-37 and I-35 are the same highway in the downtown region before I-37 veers southeast on its journey to Corpus Christi.

However, touring San Antonio is easily accomplished because, although the city is vast, most attractions are grouped in a few areas. **Downtown** sightseeing starts at **Alamo Plaza,** home of the Alamo and birthplace not only of Texas liberty but also of San Antonio tourism. Here you can take guided tours, a city bus or trolley, or just enjoy a pedestrian look at the area. Behind Alamo Plaza lies the **Paseo del Rio** or **River Walk,** one of the most visited spots in Texas. Located below street level, the river banks are lined with sidewalk cafes and specialty shops.

On one edge of the River Walk rests **La Villita,** the "little village" that was the original settlement in Old San Antonio. Here you'll find wares of many of the city's artisans displayed and sold in historic structures.

La Villita sits in the shadow of the 750-foot **Tower of the Americas,** where you can enjoy the best view of the city from the observation deck, a revolving restaurant, or the bar and disco. The tower was built as the symbol of HemisFair, the 1968 World's Fair. The tower is located in **HemisFair Park,** the grounds of the fair that now sports a fresh look following a recent facelift and addition of restful water gardens. Nearby, the **Henry B. Gonzales Convention Center** hosts thousands of conventioneers annually.

Directly south of the River Walk lies the **King William Historic District,** home of the city's stately mansions built during the 19th century. This area is a favorite for bed-and-breakfast lovers.

West of the River Walk area, a quick ride by trolley or car, is **Market Square,** the most Mexican attraction in town. Here you can shop for imports in **El Mercado** (the largest Mexican marketplace in the United States), dine on a Tex-Mex feast, or tour some nearby historic buildings.

Along **Broadway** north of downtown lie many of San Antonio's museums and outdoor attractions. **Brackenridge Park,** home of the city's zoo and Japanese gardens, along with plenty of family activities await just minutes from downtown.

Continue north on Broadway to the intersection of Loop 410, then turn west to the intersection of US 281. This is the location of the **San Antonio International Airport,** where many visitors begin and end their stay. It's also home to some of the city's best shopping areas, from big name department stores such as Saks Fifth Avenue and Marshall Field's to small import shops and art galleries.

South of downtown, the **Mission Trail** holds many attractions, especially for history buffs. Along this historic route, you can tour four Spanish missions, each still open for Sunday services.

And on the northwest side of town, along Loop 1604, lie two of Texas's top family attractions: **Fiesta Texas** and **Sea World of Texas.** From spring through fall, these parks are filled with tourists from around the U.S. and Mexico who come to enjoy thrill rides, musical productions, and marine animal shows.

STAYING COMFORTABLE

The Alamo City is a casual place, blessed with a laid-back atmosphere that casts an equally approving eye on either shorts or suits. In all but the most highbrow of establishments, you'll feel right at home in jeans, a cotton shirt, and comfortable shoes.

Much of that emphasis on comfort stems from San Antonio's weather. No matter how you look at it, now matter how long you've called this city home, San Antonio's summers can only be described as hot—*really* hot. Humidity levels runs high and the temperature even higher—averaging 95.6 in July and 95.9 in August, with 100-plus degree days not at all uncommon.

SAN ANTONIO'S COOLEST GETAWAYS

When the temperature rises, do like San Antonians do: head to someplace cool. The malls and museums of the city are cool diversions, but every Texan knows that the best way to beat the heat is to seek out water. Whether in the form of man-made water rides or natural spring-fed pools and white water rivers, splashy recreation is a winner during the sweaty days that stretch from June through September. If you just need a break from the sunshine, take a break in a cool cave. Some of the best caverns in Texas are just minutes from the Alamo City, and offer nature's air conditioning year-round.

Here's a look at the 10 coolest getaways in the San Antonio area:

Aquarena Springs and snorkeling in the San Marcos River, San Marcos (800-999-9767 or 512-396-8900; admission fee). This small, scenic theme park features Spring Lake, fed by over 200 springs that produce 150 million gallons daily. Visitors cruise on glass-bottomed boats, enjoy six rides and shows (including one featuring the park's mascot, Ralph the Swimming Pig), and view the area from the 300-foot-tall Sky Spiral. Open daily, although hours change seasonally. (While in San Marcos, you also can head down to the City Park to enjoy snorkeling in the same clear waters.)

Blue Hole, Wimberley (512-847-9127; admission fee). A favorite with locals since the area's pioneer days, this traditional Texas swimming hole comes complete with swinging ropes, tall cypress trees, and the ice-cold water of Cypress Creek. You can stay for the day and picnic on the riverbanks, or camp overnight (rustic or hookup).

Cascade Caverns, Boerne (210-755-8080; admission fee). This family-owned cavern has a 100-foot waterfall, an unusual underground sight. Guided tours take 45 minutes. For those who wish to stay longer, there's an RV park on site as well. Open daily.

Cave Without A Name, Boerne (210-537-4212; admission fee). This 50-million-year-old cave is privately owned and, while not as well known as other Hill Country caverns, boasts many beautiful formations. A 45-minute tour takes you through a series of rooms, including one with Texas-sized stalagmites. Graveled walks wind through the cavern, and no difficult climbing is necessary. Tours are given as often as visitors arrive. Call ahead. Closed Tuesdays.

Fiesta Texas water park, San Antonio (800-473-4378). With admission fee to the park, you can enjoy this water park section. Bring along a swimsuit to enjoy the "Twister," "Six Chuter," and "Gusher."

Guadalupe River rafting, New Braunfels (800-572-2626 for information on various companies; admission fee). Inner-tubers, rafters, and canoeists enjoy everything from leisurely floats to white water thrills along the Guadalupe River. River outfitters handle the equipment and the transportation, you just take care of the fun part.

Natural Bridge Caverns, New Braunfels (210-651-6101; admission fee). Named for the rock arch over the entrance, this cave is one of the most spectacular in the area. The guided tour is well lit, but the slope of the trail may be taxing for some. The cave is open year-round; phone for tour times.

Schlitterbahn, New Braunfels (400 N. Liberty, 210-625-2351; admission fee). Texas's largest water park is just a half hour from the Alamo City, and well worth the drive. This 65-acre site (the name means "slippery road" in German) is the largest tubing park in the world, with nine tube chutes, two uphill water coasters, and more than a day's worth of rides. Rides range from peaceful kiddie floats to the "Boogie Bahn," a moving mountain of water for surfing, and the "Dragon Blaster," the world's first uphill water coaster. Open May through September.

Sea World water park, San Antonio (210-523-3611). The Lost Lagoon is a five-acre park-within-a-park with rides like the "Texas Splashdown" and "Rio Loco." The newest ride is "Sky Tubin'," where up to four family members or friends link together their inner tubes for a ride down the rapids.

Splashtown, San Antonio (3600 I-35 N., 210-227-1100; admission fee). Sporting a $1.75 million renovation, this 18-acre park has dozens of slides, a kids' activity pool, a giant wave pool, and six sand volleyball courts. The newest attraction is a toboggan-style ride that churns riders along 650 feet of tube chutes. Open weekends May and September; daily during summer months.

That heat puts an emphasis on staying cool. During the summer months (and the thermometer, if not the calendar, declares that season as anytime between April and October), pack cotton. Shorts are in evidence everywhere, from attractions to restaurants, and for ladies, longer "city shorts" are frequently seen in dressier establishments.

Don't forget sunscreen. Although much of the River Walk is well shaded, the theme parks provide less break from the sun. Even 15 minutes in the sun can cause sensitive skin to burn at this southern latitude. If you'll be out during summer evenings, pack some insect repellent as well. Mosquitoes are notorious offenders during warm weather (although the purple martins that nest near the River Walk keep the numbers tolerable).

Fall in Texas is short-lived, sometimes spanning only a few weeks of long-sleeved weather before winter begins. However, winters are typically very mild, with an average high of 64.6 degrees in December, followed by 62.3 in January. While the winter is mild, do plan to bring a coat or jacket; evenings dip into the low 40s on average. Snow is very rare, occurring only once every few years. When it does fall, expect the city to come to a standstill.

Spring brings quickly warming temperatures and with it spring showers—and often thunderstorms. Flash flooding is a persistent problem in both downtown San Antonio and the surrounding Hill Country. Stay tuned to weather bulletins during heavy rains, and never drive into swiftly moving water. Every year, cars are swept off the road even in the downtown region.

IF YOU FLY IN

The San Antonio International Airport is located on the north side of town off Loop 410, approximately 15 minutes from the central downtown business district.

Airlines serving San Antonio include American, Conquest, Continental, Delta, Northwest, Southwest, TWA, United, and USAir. International flights include Aerolitoral, Aeromonterrey, Continental, and Mexicana.

Twenty-four-hour shuttle service to downtown hotels is available. For information, call (210) 366-3183 or (800) 477-0427. A shuttle ride to downtown hotels runs about $7 per person each way. A cab ride from the airport to downtown will run approximately $12 one way for up to four people.

TRANSPORTATION TIPS

San Antonio's streets, especially in the downtown area, can be confusing. Many are not perpendicular, and many are one way. Plan your route before heading out to make your journey easier.

Conventioneers and vacationers staying on the River Walk will find that a car is not a necessity. The River Walk, Convention Center, Alamo Plaza, and La Villita all lie within walking distance of each other. Parking is very limited in this area, so in many ways it's easier (and cheaper) to forgo renting a vehicle.

Instead, take a ride on the **VIA San Antonio Streetcars.** These motorized, open-air trolleys make stops at all the major hotels and attractions such as Market Square, the Alamo, the Southwest Craft Center, and the Spanish Governor's Palace. Trolleys follow four different routes that encompass just about all the downtown region. Hop aboard at any stop; fare on the trolleys is just 25 cents.

If you're traveling beyond the downtown, take a ride on a VIA, the metropolitan transit service that serves 94 routes. The most popular with travelers is the **VIA Vistas Cultural Route.** This bus stops at the missions, the Yturri-Edmunds House and Mill, the Lone Star Brewery, La Villita, the Alamo, HemisFair Plaza, the San Antonio Museum of Art, the Witte Museum, the San Antonio Zoo, the Botanical Gardens, and the McNay Museum. Rates for the VIA Vista Cultural Route are 40 cents for adults. VIA Day Tripper passes offer unlimited rides on any VIA bus or streetcar for $2. For more information on VIA, call (210) 227-2020 or visit the VIA Downtown Information Center at 112 Soledad.

GUIDED TOURS

Gray Line Tours (Reuter Bldg., 217 Alamo Plaza, 800-GRAY-LINE or 210-226-1706) offers three different San Antonio tours, all in full-sized motor coaches with professional guides. The Mission Trail tour (3 hours) provides a look at the 18th-century missions, including the Alamo. Take the Romantic San Antonio tour (3½ hours) for a look at the lush Japanese Tea Gardens, the vast collection of the McNay Art Museum, Fort Sam Houston, and the San Fernando Cathedral. Finally, the Trace of History tour (3 hours) takes in the Institute of Texan Cultures, the King William district, El Mercado, and the Lone Star Brewery.

Gray Line tours depart from Alamo Plaza. Pickup service from the downtown hotels is complimentary.

Lone Star Trolley (ticketing and boarding at Ripley's Believe It or Not! and the Plaza Theater of Wax in Alamo Plaza, 210-224-9299) gives quick overviews of the city. These red and green vehicles drive past most of San Antonio's top landmarks on the one-hour

HIDDEN TREASURES:
THE SPIRITS OF SAN ANTONIO

Behind a home built over 200 years ago, a night watchman hears the sound of a woman's cries coming from the depths of a sealed well. In a downtown hotel, employees repeatedly see a maid dressed in a uniform of the last century. And in an art center, a photographer feels a hand on his shoulder and turns to see a dark shadow in the room with him.

These are just a few examples of the spirited encounters that have occurred in San Antonio. The historic homes and museums of the Alamo City are filled with reminders of long-dead residents, ones many people believe still roam the area.

"San Antonio is a very haunted city," says Docia Williams, an author and tour guide who leads groups on night excursions of the city's "occupied" buildings. This lively lady has interviewed policemen, night watchmen, and residents of private homes throughout the city and searched the library's archives. She has gathered documented material for two ghostly tomes, *Spirits of San Antonio and South Texas* and *Ghosts Along the Texas Coast,* as well as for her "Spirits of San Antonio" bus tour (see "Guided Tours" in this section).

For a Southwestern city, San Antonio is ancient, with a long and often violent history. That's one reason Docia Williams believes there are so many supernatural occurrences. "The older the place, the more likely it is things have happened."

One of San Antonio's oldest buildings, the Alamo, is also reported to be one of the most haunted. Present-day night watchmen have heard unexplained sounds in the old mission, but the hauntings date back to the days of the historic battle. Following the battle, Mexican soldiers were said to have run from the Alamo shouting *"diablos"* (devils). The reference could have been to their opponents—or to some other presence in the mission.

Another story deals with the order that was issued to burn the Alamo following the Battle of San Jacinto. Soldiers entered the old building but soon fled, refusing to carry out their mission. Their leader came to speak to the men. Entering the building, he was met by six ghosts holding swords of fire—rumored to be the ghosts of the Spanish priests who built the Alamo.

The priests who haunt the Alamo are in the company of nuns

not far away at the Southwest Craft Center, located at 300 Augusta at Navarro. Today a gallery and working studio for many San Antonio craftsmen, the building was once a girls' school run by cloistered nuns.

"The only men ever allowed here were the doctor, if someone were very ill, and the parish priest who said the mass on Sunday," says Williams. "No other men were allowed. Now there are all these male teachers and security guards."

So from a ghost's point of view, it's not surprising that some strange occurrences have taken place. "The photography teacher was in the darkroom not too long ago, and he came out and felt a hand on his shoulder kind of shoving him," says the tour guide. "He turned around and there was nothing but a dark shadow. About a month or so later, the same thing happened to him, but this time it was a misty white shadow." The dark shadow was explained as a nun's habit, but what about the white apparition? That second incident took place in the summer, a time when the nuns of the school always changed into a white habit.

Several San Antonio museums are rumored to be haunted. The Institute of Texan Cultures supposedly is haunted by the ghost of its former director, a pipe smoker. Williams says late-night employees still report smelling his tobacco smoke. And, when night watchmen make their rounds, they often find the doors of the hearse in the Castroville exhibit mysteriously open. They close the hearse doors, make their rounds, and return to find them open once again.

Another allegedly haunted museum is the Jose Navarro house at 228 South Laredo, home of one of the signers of the Texas Declaration of Independence. Located next to the jail, the home is said to have cold spots, rocking chairs that move without human help, and furniture that rearranges itself. Not far away, at the Spanish Governor's Palace built in 1749, the spirit of a former servant allegedly haunts the home. The woman was killed by robbers, and her body was thrown into a well behind the home. Today the well is capped, but night guards still report hearing her moans, says Williams.

Although the itinerary of Docia Williams's "Spirits of San Antonio" tour changes, one thing remains constant: all tours are conducted at night. The reason is simple, she says. "No self-respecting ghost would be out in daylight."

tour. The Alamo, El Mercado, the Spanish Governor's Palace, La Villita, the Tower of the Americas, the Institute of Texan Cultures, and more are featured on the drive-by narrated tour conducted by very knowledgeable guides.

Texas Trolley (Alamo Visitors Center, 210-228-9776 or 225-8587) offers one-hour narrated tour cruises by many downtown attractions, including HemisFair Park, La Villita, the San Fernando Cathedral, the King William district, El Mercado, and the Alamo.

San Antonio City Tours (Alamo Visitors Center, 210-520-TOUR) takes visitors on a mini-city tour for a 90-minute look at Mission Concepción, the King William Historic District, and the Japanese Gardens. Half-day tours include the Alamo, the Lone Star Brewery, and El Mercado; the Grand Tour adds in a riverboat ride, the Institute of Texan Cultures, the IMAX theater, and lunch at the historic Menger Hotel. Tours depart from the Alamo Visitors Center, and pickup service at downtown hotels is complimentary.

Look for the pink buses sporting black sombreros (*only* in San Antonio) and you'll see the **Fiesta City Fun Tours** (southwest corner of the Alamo, 210-533-5398). These tours take in most popular downtown attractions include the Alamo, the Spanish Governor's Palace, Market Square, and the King William district.

For a different side of the city, consider a **"Spirits of San Antonio" Tour** (210-493-2454). These nighttime ventures take in San Antonio's "haunted" buildings, from the Menger Hotel to the Alamo to the Spanish Governor's Palace. Tours run for groups only, but guide Docia Williams keeps a list of interested individuals and plans a tour when she has 20 participants.

TEXAS CUISINE

While Easterners were sitting down to meals seasoned with imported spices and served on fine china, Texas was still a frontier. Throughout much of its history as part of Mexico, then as an independent republic, and finally as a state, Texas remained a vast land sparsely populated by cowboys and hardy pioneer types who learned to cook using the materials they had at hand, whether that meant finding a use for prickly pear pads or rangy beef as tough as shoe leather.

Today San Antonio boasts fine restaurants serving *haute cuisine* and Continental fare. But the real treasure lies in the dishes that either originated in Texas or came here to be perfected, dishes that serve as reminders of frontier ingenuity like fajitas and chicken-fried steak, plus ethnic favorites like German sausage and Tex-Mex enchiladas.

The designation "Tex-Mex" refers to the particular style of Mexican food found in the Lone Star State. Unlike New Mexico's Mexican food, which might include blue corn tortillas, or California Mexican food that relies on avocados and black olives, Tex-Mex depends heavily on ground beef, cheese, and chili sauce.

Texas specialties have two things in common. First, most can trace their roots to harder times, when it was a necessity to use every cut of meat, even some that more gentrified diners might consider scrap; second, Texans rely on beef. Cattle are king here, and beef makes an appearance on every menu and at every backyard cookout. Since the cowboy days, beef has taken Texas diners by the horns (or at least the silverware) and led them to a table set with everything from T-bone to ground beef.

Those early cowboy cooks knew that not all meat was steak; some of it was tough and even stringy. They used Western ingenuity to turn what could have been waste into dishes that award-winning restaurants are now proud to serve. Chicken-fried steak is such a dish, using one of the toughest cuts of meat: the round steak. It's tenderized (the cook just beats the meat into submission), dipped in an egg and milk batter, and then floured and fried to a golden crispiness.

The chicken-fried steak is the equivalent of white bread in Texas cuisine. Folks feel comfortable with chicken-fried steak. It's not spicy, so even those who can't handle the fiery heat of other local dishes love this one. Usually served drowned in a wave of white gravy, it's even a favorite with children, who look for it in the form of nuggets or "steak fingers" on kids' menus across the state. When you place your order, just ask for "a chicken fried." Expect to be served a huge platter overflowing with the steak plus a fat slab of Texas toast and two vegetables, often French fries and fried okra.

When you're ready for something spicier, order up the state dish of Texas: chili. In the 1880s, young girls known as "chili queens" sold *chili con carne* from kiosks in San Antonio's Market Square. When the dish went to the Chicago World's Fair in 1893, chili caught on and the rest, as they say, is history. Although health ordinances closed down the chili queens' operation in 1937, chili con carne is now sold in various degrees of spiciness that range from warm to explosive.

Fajitas are a favorite "trash to treasure" Tex-Mex treat. Fajitas were a brainstorm of chuck wagon cooks who learned that marinating the tough skirt steak in lime juice broke down the meat into chewable consistency. Sliced in narrow strips and grilled, it is now served with cheese, salsa, and guacamole, and rolled into a flour tortilla. Restaurants like to toss the meat onto a hot metal platter with a squirt of lime juice, sending up enough fragrant fajita smoke to make everyone around wish they had ordered this smoky wonder. Pair that with a basket of warm tortilla chips, a bowl of Pace picante sauce (San Antonio's own), and a salt-rimmed margarita (invented just south of the Rio Grande), and you're in Tex-Mex heaven.

As you check out the fajita offerings, you'll spot not just beef but also chicken and shrimp. Don't be fooled by their designation as fajitas. The only true fajitas are beef; the others are simply grilled meat. (OK, they taste great, but just don't call them fajitas.)

You can find great chicken enchiladas with a flavorful *verde* tomatillo sauce as well as vegetarian dishes and even shrimp enchiladas. But the real Tex-Mex favorite, known affectionately as "Regular Plate No. 1," is an order of beef enchiladas, refried beans, and Spanish rice. If you're lucky, *leche quemada,* a sugary pecan praline, will be brought out with your check.

Tamales, both mild and spicy varieties, are also found on every Tex-Mex menu, but they're most popular during the Christmas season. Making tamales at home is a time-consuming job, one traditionally tackled by large families. Tamales start with the preparation of a hog's head, boiled with garlic, spices, peppers, and cilantro. After cooking, the meat is ground and then simmered with spices. As the filling is prepared, other family members ready the *hojas* or corn husks used to wrap the tamale. Others prepare the *masa,* a cornmeal worked with lard and seasonings that is spread thinly on the shucks before filling with meat. Finally, the tamales are steamed in huge pots.

Some special menu items are found in restaurants frequented by locals rather than tourists. One of these dishes is *cabrito,* tender young goat usually cooked over an open flame on a spit. *Cabrito* is a common dish in border towns, where you can often see it hanging on spits in market windows.

All this spicy food makes a diner plenty thirsty. The traditional Texas drink, one enjoyed by some at breakfast, lunch, and dinner, is iced tea. Want a soft drink? Dr. Pepper, invented by a Waco pharmacist, is a popular favorite. Beer goes hand-in-hand with Tex-Mex, from Texas products like Lone Star and Pearl to Mexican brands like Dos Equis, Corona, and Tecate.

If you go overboard with the beer, the Tex-Mex cure the next

A DINER'S GUIDE TO MEXICAN FOOD

BUÑELOS—cinnamon crisps served as a dessert.

BOTANAS—appetizers.

CABRITO—young, tender goat.

CERVEZA—beer.

CHALUPA—fried, flat corn tortilla spread with refried beans and topped with meat, lettuce, tomatoes, and cheese; open-faced taco.

CHICARRONES—fried pork cracklings.

CHILE RELLENOS—stuffed peppers.

CHORIZO—spicy pork sausage.

ENCHILADA—corn or flour tortillas wrapped around a filled and covered with a hot or mild sauce; varieties include beef, chicken, cheese, sour cream, and shrimp.

FAJITA—grilled skirt steak strips, wrapped in flour tortillas and usually served still sizzling on a metal platter with condiments (*pico de gallo*, sour cream, cheese) on the side.

FLAUTA—corn tortillas wrapped around beef, chicken, or pork and fried until crispy; may be an appetizer or an entree.

FRIJOLES REFRITOS—refried beans.

GUACAMOLE—avocado dip spiced with chopped onions, peppers, and herbs.

HUEVOS RANCHEROS—ranch-style eggs, spicy and made with tomatoes and chiles.

LECHE QUEMADA—pecan praline made with burnt sugar; the number one dessert in Tex-Mex restaurants.

MARGARITA—popular tequila drink, served in a salted glass either over ice or frozen.

MENUDO—soup made from tripe.

MIGAS—eggs scrambled with torn strips of corn tortillas.

MOLE (pronounced "MOLE-ay")—an unusual sauce made with nuts, spices, and chocolate; served over chicken enchiladas.

PICANTE SAUCE—red sauce made from peppers and onions, and eaten as dip for tortilla chips; ranges from mild to very hot.

PICO DE GALLO—hot sauce made of chopped onions, peppers, and cilantro.

QUESADILLA—tortilla covered with cheese and baked.

SOPAPILLA—fried pastry dessert served with honey.

Continued

TAMALE—corn dough filled with chopped pork, rolled in a corn shuck, and steamed; served with or without chile sauce.

TORTILLA—flat bread-like disc made of flour or corn; used to make many main dishes, and also served as an accompaniment to the meal, with or without butter.

TOSTADA—fried tortilla.

VERDE—green sauce, used as a dip or on enchiladas.

morning is a bowl of *menudo*. This spicy soup, made from tripe, is a popular hangover remedy. It's sold in restaurants, and canned versions are even sold in grocery stores throughout San Antonio.

Although Texas cuisine borrows heavily from the Mexican culture, it also relies on other ethnic groups that settled this land. Over 30 nationalities, from Alsatians to Czechs to Poles, settled communities throughout Texas, bringing their own culinary styles and adjusting them to fit the food supply they found on the frontier.

The Germans, one of the largest immigrant groups, were very influential in San Antonio and brought with them the dishes of their homeland. One area museum explains that when German farmers butchered a pig, they "used everything but the squeal." Some shoppers preferred not to see those parts looking back at them across a meat counter, so the German meat markets used whatever didn't sell to make sausage. Today sausage is a top draw in barbecue joints across the state.

Barbecue is found throughout San Antonio, in side-of-the-road joints and even sit-down restaurants with cloth napkins. Beef rules, although you'll find a good selection of pork ribs, chicken, ham, and even *cabrito* rounding out the offerings.

Barbecue ranks with state politics when it comes to provoking heated discussion between Texans. One barbecue joint has a sign over its counter that says it best: "Bar-b-que, sex and death are subjects that provoke intense speculation in most Texans. Out of the three, probably bar-b-que is taken most seriously."

For dessert, try flan, a caramel-colored custard. Or stick with that Southern favorite, pecan pie, to finish off a real Texas meal. (Feel those arteries slam shut yet?)

PROFESSIONAL SPORTS TEAMS

No matter when you visit San Antonio, somewhere someone is

playing professional sports. From hoops to hockey, there's plenty of team action to keep sports-lovers occupied:

BASKETBALL

San Antonio Spurs Basketball (NBA), 100 Montana, San Antonio, TX 78203; (210) 554-7787

BASEBALL

San Antonio Missions Baseball, P. O. Box 28268, San Antonio, TX 78228; (210) 675-PARK
San Antonio Tejanos, P. O. Box 791611, San Antonio, TX 78279-1611; (210) 434-5266

HOCKEY

San Antonio Iguanas (Central Hockey League), 110 Broadway, Suite 25, San Antonio, TX 78205; (210) 227-4449

SOCCER

San Antonio Pumas (South Central Professional Soccer League), 4922 Fredericksburg Rd., San Antonio, TX 78229; (210) 223-5425

ADDITIONAL INFORMATION SOURCES

The richest source of information here is the **Visitor Information Center** (317 Alamo Plaza), operated by the San Antonio Convention and Visitors Bureau. It is located directly across from the Alamo at 317 Alamo Plaza.

The **San Antonio Convention and Visitors Bureau** also operates a toll free line: (800) 447-3372. Call to order a free visitors packet, get information on convention delegate housing, or to obtain information on specific attractions.

A tourist information center is also located at the Menger Hotel. The **Alamo Visitor Center** (216 Alamo Plaza, 210-225-8587) provides brochures on area attractions and sells tickets for the IMAX, San Antonio City Tours, the Texas Trolley, the riverboat rides, Sea World of Texas, and Fiesta Texas. Tours aboard the San Antonio City Tours buses and the Texas Trolley also depart from here.

For 24-hour information on shopping, attractions, dining, transportation, and weather, as well as concerts, special events, Hill Country day trips, and banking, call the **free information line** at

(210) 732-INFO. You can also make reservations after hearing recorded information.

Disability accessibility information can be obtained by calling (210) 207-7243 or, for TDD users, (210) 207-7911.

Foreign currency exchange is available at the San Antonio International Airport. Call (210) 824-7329 for information.

The Mexican Consulate's office is located at 127 Navarro. For information, call (210) 227-9145.

How To Use This Guide

This is a book for San Antonio vacationers and conventioneers—folks looking for a good meal, a good shop, a good night's sleep, and a good time in the most popular vacation spot in Texas. This is not an exhaustive guide to the Alamo City, but rather one that we feel covers places that make San Antonio unique.

Although long-time Texans, we are not San Antonio residents. We are what you are—San Antonio vacationers. Yes, we may be several hundred visits ahead of you, but we still recall the excitement of discovering this special city. The history, the romance, and the atmosphere keep us coming back for more.

And, as vacationers, we feel that we're especially qualified to write a vacation guide to this special city. Our journeys to San Antonio are like fairy tales where everyone lives happily ever after. We never have to worry about the school system or the city council or the hundreds of other details that weigh down our view of where we live. Instead, we come to San Antonio for a good time, for unbeatable atmosphere, and for long, unhurried meals followed by longer strolls down the winding river.

To make the most of your visit, first do a little pre-trip planning. In what area of the city will you be staying? Will you need transportation or can you walk and rely on city trolleys? What are you most interested in visiting? This guide can help you answer those questions.

Second, be flexible. Travel is a journey of discovery that may take you down a different—and possibly more interesting—route than the one you originally intended. If your River Walk visit coincides with Fiesta, for instance, your stay will be shared with hundreds of thousands of other visitors. Things will take a little longer; your total number of stops may be a little fewer. But at the same time, you'll be joining in on gaiety and festivity that makes this city distinct.

This guide is divided geographically with subsections on attractions, shopping, dining, and accommodations in each area. Again, it's not a comprehensive listing, but a selection of the places we felt were special.

Rather than list specific hours and admission fee prices, both of which change more often than Texas weather, we've listed the phone number for the establishments. Call ahead of your visit and check on times and cost to avoid unpleasant surprises. Also, numerous San Antonio attractions are free and are listed as such, but many accept and encourage donations.

Rather than list specific prices for restaurants, we've adopted a dollar sign system:

$ = Inexpensive ($5 and under)

$$ = Moderate ($5 to $15)

$$$ = Expensive (over $15)

Similarly, we've also listed price ranges for accommodations for a standard room:

$ = Inexpensive (under $100)

$$ = Moderate ($100 to $150)

$$$ = Expensive (over $150)

The symbol □ denotes credit card acceptance.

Although we could not go into a great deal of detail on every attraction, we've featured several unique spots in "Hidden Treasures" sections sprinkled throughout the book. These are aimed at introducing you to some lesser known spots.

No guide can be everything for every reader. Your own best judgment must prevail. Keep in mind your own limits, and make your plans accordingly. Be aware of the conditions around you, and be flexible enough to adjust to meet those conditions.

With these tips in mind, let the trip begin. Whether you're journeying from your armchair or the driver's seat, we hope the following pages will help you to enjoy the Alamo City.

River Walk

The Paseo del Rio, or River Walk, is a magical place 20 feet below street level. Nestled behind tall buildings, away from traffic and street noise, the River Walk is the most popular spot in town, lined with specialty shops and European-style *al fresco* cafes. Visitors stroll the walkways that follow the winding river. Some sections throng with visitors shoulder-to-shoulder; others have a quiet, almost park-like atmosphere.

Today the River Walk is the heart of the city. Tourists from around the world pack the hotels here. Military personnel from San Antonio's five bases (four Air Force and one Army) enjoy a few hours off duty at the outdoor cafes. And locals, lifelong San Antonians, come to the area to enjoy a respite from the hustle and bustle of the city.

But its popularity goes back far before the days when people came here for sizzling fajitas and frozen margaritas. Payaya Indians called this river *Yanaguana,* or "refreshing waters." It also had a less elegant nickname—"a drunken old man going home at night"—in reference to its numerous twists and turns. Indians camped along the river banks and hunted on the rich land nearby.

On June 13, 1691, the feast day of San Antonio de Padua, the Spanish renamed the Yanaguana. The change was just a hint at the many transformations the river would soon witness as Spanish domination came to the area.

In the early 1700s, the Spaniards constructed missions on the river's bends. The northernmost site was built first: San Antonio de Valero, later known as the Alamo. It was followed by four other missions to the south. The Indians who lived in the missions dug ditches or *acequias* from the river to their fields to irrigate crops of beans and corn.

Soon settlement began on the riverbanks. When the missions were secularized and later occupied by military troops, camp followers and tradesman built temporary houses near the river to serve those stationed at the Alamo. After Texas became a republic, permanent settlements developed on the riverbanks. As the population rose, bathhouses sprang up along the water's edge.

The condition of the river declined, and for many residents its only characteristics were bad. The river was untamed and in the downtown area it wreaked havoc after heavy rains. In 1921, a devastating flood killed 50 people, and talk was that the river should be covered with concrete and converted to a storm sewer. But on March 22, 1924, the San Antonio Conservation Society stepped in to prevent the river from being converted in this way.

The river was saved with a puppet show called "The Goose That Laid the Golden Egg." Cloth puppets resembling city officials dramatized the tale and helped San Antonians realize that their river really could be a golden egg. A flood control program was started, and dams were built to protect the horseshoe bend during floods.

While the river was saved, the real gold came later, thanks to a visionary named Robert H. H. Hugman. As part of a WPA program, Hugman was commissioned to develop the scenic walkway. He pictured a festive area he called "The Shops of Aragon and Romula," named for the cities of Old Spain.

But development along the River Walk remained minimal until the World HemisFair. In the late 1960s, preparing for global visitors, the city beautified the park, investors opened businesses along the walkways, and the River Walk, as visitors today now know and love it, was born.

Finally the River Walk had attained what Hugman had envisioned over half a century before. The latter once wrote that he wanted the river "considered as a stage setting on which people are transported to the unusual. Unusual shops, unusual landscaping, color and modes of transportation. The greatest need for the future is to not go modern in architectural styles, but to guard jealously the river tempo, slow and lazy, in complete contrast with the hustle and bustle of street level modern city life." Any visitor would agree that Hugman's wishes have been wonderfully accomplished.

No matter what day of the week, no matter what time of the year you visit, activity abounds along the River Walk. This is where city residents come to party, where conventioneers come to meet, and where vacationers come to taste the flavor that is San Antonio.

The River Walk spans 2½ miles from Municipal Auditorium to the north to King William Historic District to the south. For the best overview, take a ride on a river barge, a narrated tour that provides a look at stretches most pedestrians never see.

One of the northernmost attractions on the River Walk is the Southwest Craft Center (see "Attractions" in this section). Formerly a convent, the nuns sequestered here from the outside world once relied on the water of the river.

From the Craft Center, the river winds below numerous bridges (35 in all), each different in style. It flows on past several hotels and finally reaches the floodgates that mark the beginning of the horseshoe bend, the U-shaped section that makes up 50 percent of the walkway but a far greater percentage of the River Walk businesses and visitors. Here the river is uniformly shallow—about four feet deep throughout.

Turning east, you'll soon reach La Mansion del Rio Hotel and one of the quietest stretches of the river. Here you can enjoy lush vegetation maintained by city crews. Seventy-five types of trees line the walkways, from banana and cypress to colorful crepe myrtle.

Next to La Mansion stands the Nix Medical Center, built in 1929. Today it supplies medicinal help in the form of mixed drinks and buckets of shrimp and fries at Dick's Last Resort, housed on the lowest level.

The bank opposite this stretch was vacant for many years, but today it boasts San Antonio's newest development. Called the South Bank, this entertainment and retail complex has the River Walk's hottest new spot—the Hard Rock Cafe—plus other favorites such as Paesano's, Fat Tuesday's, County Line Barbecue, Howl at the Moon, and, soon, Planet Hollywood. The South Bank is now one of the most popular nightspots on the river.

As you round the bend, you'll be heading into the most commercial stretch of the river. Starting with the Hyatt Regency Hotel, a property that trenched an extension of the river throughout its lobby and into water gardens beyond, and all the way to the Arneson River Theatre, the River Walk is packed. Here the crowds thicken and sometimes form an endless queue that moves along the flagstone path.

Along this main stretch, every kind of shop and restaurant awaits, all in the shade of towering cypress trees. If you turn east from here, either passing through the Hyatt lobby or rising up to street level at a corner, you'll be in Alamo Plaza.

At the intersection of Commerce Street, marked by the Casa Rio restaurant (the first business on the River Walk), the river makes a turn. This is a man-made strip; you won't find shops along this stretch, just hundreds of cypress "knees" that look like stools for leprechauns and a man-made waterfall. Here also stands a statue of San Antonio de Padua, the city's patron saint.

At the end of the walk, the river forks. Head south and you'll be at the Henry B. Gonzales Convention Center. Beyond this lies HemisFair Park (always in sight because of its 750-foot Tower of the Americas).

On the north side is the Rivercenter Mall, a shopping center that's an attraction in its own right. Architects married the mall and the river, creating a union that is a delight even for non-shoppers.

Return to the main stretch of the river and continue south, beyond the Hilton to the Arneson River Theatre. You'll see the grass-covered steps that serve as seats for the audience that sits across the river from the stage. During paid performances, you may have to go up and into La Villita to get around the Arneson and continue on your river journey.

Beyond the river theater, the crowds again slack off. The river travels through the elegant King William Historic District and past the Pioneer Flour Mills (once powered by the water's force).

ATTRACTIONS

The most popular activity for vacationers in the River Walk area is a leisurely cruise on a **river barge** (210-222-1701; admission fee). These flat boats with four rows of bench seating provide narrated tours along the Paseo del Rio. Tours last slightly over half an hour and depart from one of two points: opposite the Hilton Palacio del Rio and at the Rivercenter Mall. Each covers the same route.

You'll notice many boats set up with dining tables and filled with diners enjoying a meal from a River Walk eatery. To dine on a barge, contact the restaurants themselves, not the river boat ticket offices. These boats are rented by groups, but some restaurants fill in vacancies with walk-ins.

The northern section of the river, beyond where most pedestrians ever stroll, is the home of the **Southwest Craft Center** (300 Augusta St., 210-224-1848; free). Here you'll find a good overview of the San Antonio arts and crafts scene. The Center is housed in the former Ursuline Academy, which in 1851 became the first girls' school in the city. The long halls of the once busy dormitory are now filled with studios—photography, jewelry, fibers, paper making, painting, and the like. The Ursuline Gift Shop sells hand-crafted items, including silver Southwestern jewelry, hand-painted plates, and wooden Christmas ornaments. Grab a sandwich or salad at the Craft Center's Copper Kitchen, or some sweets at the Garden Room.

At the south end of the River Walk, just beyond the Hilton Palacio del Rio, sits the **Arneson River Theatre** (418 Villita St., 210-299-8610). This unique theater was erected in 1939, designed by River Walk architect Robert Hugman and built by the WPA. Have a seat on the grass-covered steps and enjoy a look at a San Antonio institution. In this open-air format, the river, not a curtain, separates performers from the audience. Some of San Antonio's top events take place here, including Fiesta Noche del Rio, a summer show that has been in operation nearly four decades (see "Festivals" at the back of the book for more information).

Shows of a more high-tech nature are the draw at the **IMAX Theater** (849 E. Commerce at Rivercenter Mall, 210-225-4629; admission fee). The story of the fall of the Alamo comes to life on this six-story screen several times daily. The 45-minute docudrama is one of the best film versions of the 13-day siege, giving viewers a real sense of participation in the action. The film was produced at Alamo Village in the West Texas town of Brackettville, using a replica of the Alamo built for the John Wayne film of the same name. From a rolling thunderstorm over the rugged Texas landscape to the daybreak siege by Santa Anna's troops, this movie makes viewers feel as if they are witnessing the fateful battle and the days leading up to it. When not running "The Price of Freedom," the IMAX shows other films produced especially for the big screen.

For entertainment of an older order, stop by the **Hertzberg Circus Museum** (210 Market St., 210-299-7810; admission fee). One of the largest circusiana collections in the world, this unusual museum contains more than 20,000 items of big top memorabilia, including antique circus posters, Tom Thumb's miniature carriage, and a scale model of a three-ring circus.

SHOPPING

Rivercenter Mall (849 E. Commerce) contains over 150 specialty shops and big-name department stores, as well as many restaurants. The Marriott Rivercenter Hotel soars from one arm of the structure. One of the most attractive shopping malls in the nation, Rivercenter stretches out over one million square feet encased in aqua-colored glass, giving shoppers a lovely view of the River Walk. Although the shopping is nice, the real attraction of the Rivercenter Mall is the river. A new arm of the San Antonio River was trenched out and extended into the U-shaped mall to bring the River Walk into the shopping center. The two sides of the mall are connected by the Bridge Market. Patterned after Italy's Ponte Vecchio, this area of the structure is filled with artisans selling their work.

Entertainment takes place throughout the day at the mall's outdoor performance island. As river taxis lazily cruise past, singers and dancers entertain shoppers and diners. On weekends, visitors

HIDDEN TREASURES:
UNDER THE BIG TOP

The circus is coming to town! The original mass entertainment, the circus has delighted all ages since the first performance near London in 1768. Twenty-five years later, the circus came to this country, and since then small town sideshows and big tent arenas have thrilled Americans with clowns, acrobats, and animals. This bit of history has been saved for generations to come at the Hertzberg Circus Museum, located one block off the River Walk.

The Hertzberg holds the distinction of being the oldest circus museum in the country, and one of the most important collections of circus memorabilia. It was opened to the public in 1942, two years after the death of former Texas state senator Harry Hertzberg. Senator Hertzberg had been acquiring circusiana since the 1920s, and he was one of the most avid collectors of his day. Today researchers also use the museum's library sources, such as newspaper clippings, scrapbooks, and genealogical records, to learn more about specific circuses and performers. But the real aim of the museum is just fun and enjoyment for visitors of all ages.

As you open the front doors, you almost expect to hear the booming voice of the ringmaster, smell the sawdust floor, and taste the sweetness of cotton candy. Instead, you're greeted by a grandiose parade wagon decorated with ornate gold elephants and leopards. Used by the Gentry Bros. circus in 1902, this wagon once served as a ticket booth.

General Tom Thumb's carriages, located in the next room, are some of the museum's most prized exhibits. Forty inches tall, Charles Sherwood Stratton (better known as Tom Thumb) made appearances in one of the carriages pulled by small ponies. His wife, Lavinia Warren, later used this carriage after her husband's death in 1883. The museum also has the small carriage Tom Thumb used at the age of five. Other reminders of this famous couple include a piece of their 1863 wedding cake, a miniature rifle, and a tiny violin.

The museum also features displays on sideshow acts. The collection once belonged to David Navarro, a circus fat boy himself in the 1880s and 1890s. The exhibit includes photos of performers such as Lucia Zarate, the smallest woman who ever lived.

Born in San Carlos, Mexico, in 1864, Zarate stood under 20 inches tall at maturity and weighed no more than five pounds. In the same room, displays remember Jack Earle, the "Texas Giant" who stood 8½ feet tall.

Step through the curtain in the sideshow room to take a peek under the big top. A full-fledged circus, complete with bleachers, animals, trapeze artists, and sideshow acts, awaits. There's only one catch—the "big" top is only about nine feet long, the ringmaster a little larger than a thimble, and the wooden poles the size of straws. Every piece is made to scale, a replica of the tented railroad circuses of the 1920s and 1930s. Built by ringmaster Colonel Harry Thomas, the project took 15 years to complete.

Although you may think the figures in the miniature circus are tiny, have a look at the second-floor exhibit on flea circuses to see true Lilliputian proportions. The Chapeau Circus, so named because it was stored in the hat of its owner, dates back to the early 1900s. It boasted two acts: Phillipe the Phantom Phlea and Caroline. Phillipe was an escape artist who, after being tied to a chair and locked in a safe, could reappear in a small padlocked trunk. Caroline performed on a wire and also on a bicycle.

Brook's Circus, assembled in Great Britain shortly after World War II, was a three-act flea circus that traveled in a miniature suitcase. Florence La Flea performed as gymnast and contortionist, dancing on the head of a pin. Percy Phlea drew crowds with his "Dive of Death," plunging into a single drop of water after being set on fire. In the grand finale, Afton Caliber, "The Cannon Ball Flea," was fired from a compressed-air miniature cannon onto a target two inches away.

Not to be outdone, the Armadillo Penny Matchbox Circus featured four acts, all in a matchbox. For one penny, onlookers could watch the Strong Man Flea, the Unicyclist, the Ball Walker, and even the High Diving Flea.

---

can look forward to anything from lively mariachi music to singers performing rousing Texas tunes.

For Texas souvenirs in the mall, stop by **The Texas Shop at Dillard's** (210-227-4343). Dillard's is housed in the former Joske's department store, known for generations as "The Big Store" to South Texas shoppers. When Rivercenter was constructed, the existing store formed the cornerstone for the modern mall. The Texas Shop has Texas-themed merchandise, from T-shirts to stylish Southwestern fashions. Also in the mall, **Guitars and Cadillacs** (210-224-9821) offers a wide array of Lone Star State merchandise, from specialty foods to shirts and jewelry.

Wine enthusiasts should save time for a stop at **Blum Street Cellars** (Rivercenter Mall at Blum Street, 210-222-BLUM). This shop specializes in Texas wines plus an assortment of Lone Star State specialty foods and gift items. They even offer chilled wines, so you can take a bottle back to your hotel room or enjoy it with a picnic lunch.

Shops line the main stretch of the River Walk as well, most specializing in souvenirs that range from Mexican imports to Texas specialty foods. One of the best selections of Southwest and Mexican folk art and furniture is found at **Santa Fe Connection** (231 Losoya, 210-224-5353). Located at street level next to the Lone Star Cafe, this shop boasts a huge inventory of imports from Mexico and Central and South America in all price ranges.

The artwork comes from a little closer to home at the **Texas Trails Gallery** (245 Losoya, 210-224-7865). All mediums are explored in this fine arts gallery, from watercolors to woodwork. Especially notable are the delicate bird carvings by James Middleton that portray many Texas species.

Another busy shopping area is the Kangaroo/River Square area. Here you'll find **We Three** (518 River Walk, 210-229-1164), a collection of Texas gourmet foods, cookbooks, collectibles, cowboy kitsch, and clothing. Nearby at **Santa's Christmas Shoppe Inc.** (508 River Walk, 210-222-2117), it's always Christmas—even when the San Antonio heat has visitors moving at a crawl.

DINING

AMERICAN

One of the rowdiest places on the river is **Dick's Last Resort** (406 Navarro St., 210-224-0026; $–$$, □). This is the sort of place where the waiters and waitresses like to crack jokes and toss out matchbooks sporting old photos of topless women, plus the ladies' room is decorated with photos of scantily clad hunks and vending machines offering fluorescent condoms. The restaurant offers both inside and outside seating. If you dine inside, plan to sit at huge communal tables and enjoy an earful of good blues played by some of the area's finest musicians. The menu here leans toward barbecue, but includes choices from burgers to chicken to shrimp. Everything is served in small tin buckets on a tablecloth of white butcher paper. Main dishes arrive with a bucket of french fries and bread. Save room for the desserts: Mississippi mud pie, cheesecake, and that Texas favorite, pecan pie.

Popular around the globe, San Antonio now has its own **Hard Rock Cafe** (111 Crockett St., 210-224-7625; $$, □). Part of the new South Bank development project, the Hard Rock Cafe is filled with rock 'n roll memorabilia, good old American food, and, of course, the popular Hard Rock Cafe gift shop selling the requisite T-shirts. Southeby's says that Hard Rock Cafe has the most extensive collection of rock memorabilia in the world, so stop by and have a look for yourself.

ASIAN

Hunan River Garden (506 River Walk, 210-222-0808; $–$$, □) offers up traditional Chinese fare, from sweet-and-sour pork to Kung Pao chicken, with a view that's definitely *non*-traditional.

BARBECUE

The County Line (111 Crockett St., 210-229-1941; $$, □) is an institution among Texas barbecue lovers—folks who know good barbecue. With locations around the state, this restaurant is a step above the usual BBQ joint, the kind of place where you might go to celebrate a special event with some special food. Like the other locations, this County Line specializes in slow-cooked barbecue. Have your table order the all-you-can-eat extravaganza and you'll feast on beef ribs, brisket, and sausage served family style, with huge bowls of sour cream potato salad, crunchy coleslaw, and tasty pintos. The side dishes are made from scratch daily. There's even homemade bread that rises twice before baking.

CAJUN

If you're hungry for filé gumbo or oysters on the half shell, head to **The Bayous Riverside** (517 N. Presa, 210-223-6403; $$, □). This restaurant is located right on the banks of the river, and serves up spicy Cajun fare, including shrimp remoulade. Upstairs, the **Presa St. Cafe** (210-223-6434; $–$$, □) is an oyster bar serving Cajun and casual foods. Along with spicy shrimp and oysters, the menu includes burgers and tacos. Enjoy your dinner here with live entertainment nightly.

DELI

Schilo's Delicatessen (428 E. Commerce St., 210-223-6692; $, □) is located on the street, not on the River Walk, but what it lacks in atmosphere it definitely makes up for in history. The deli was founded by Papa Fritz Schilo, a German immigrant. He opened a saloon in 1917, but when Prohibition came along he converted the operation to a deli. It was a lucky break for diners; mere suds could never match the subs and sandwiches that keep this deli packed with locals. Try a Reuben or a ham and cheese, or go all out for dinner with entrees like *wienerschnitzel* or bratwurst.

FAST FOOD

If you just want to grab a quick bite, head to the **Food Court** in the lower level of the Rivercenter Mall. Everything from chicken to Chinese and burgers to baked potatoes is available. There's plenty of seating inside, but if the weather is nice get a riverside table. This is the cheapest meal you'll find on the riverbanks and a great spot for families on a budget.

ITALIAN

The taste of Italy, from calamari to capellini with shrimp and scallops, comes to the River Walk at **Michelino's** (521 River Walk, 210-223-2939; $$, □). Pasta dishes and pizzas are offered along with more elegant fare, such as grilled pork tenderloin with foccacia bread and fine wine.

For Italian with more of a fast food pace, head to **Pieca d'Italia** (502 River Walk, 210-227-5511; $, □). This casual restaurant serves up chicken Romano, lasagna, or vegetarian stomboli as well as many low-fat selections. Pull a chair under one of this restaurant's umbrella-shaded tables and enjoy the parade of pedestrians.

SOUTHWESTERN

Ask many San Antonians for their favorite River Walk eatery, and you'll hear the name **Boudro's** (421 River Walk, 210-224-8484; $$, □). This steak and seafood restaurant offers the finest in Southwestern cuisine, usually with a twist that makes it unique even among San Antonio's plethora of excellent eateries. Start with a cactus margarita, a frozen concoction with a jolt of red cactus liqueur. Follow that eye-opener with an appetizer of smoked chicken or crab quesadillas or crab and shrimp tamales. Save room, though, for Boudro's specialties—coconut shrimp, pecan grilled fish fillet, or the specialty of the house, blackened prime rib. Seating is available on the River Walk or in the dining room.

Zuni Bar and Grill (511 River Walk, 210-227-0864; $$, □) also serves Southwestern cuisine to River Walk diners, with selections that start with blue corn nachos and andouille and brie quesadillas and then progress to specials such as roasted poblano pepper filled with shrimp and mozzarella and spicy fajitas served with black beans.

SPORTS BARS

Whether it's to watch sports or to be surrounded by sports memorabilia, folks head to **Champions of San Antonio** (849 E. Commerce in the Rivercenter Mall, 210-226-7171; $, □). After an appetizer of quesadillas, tackle a Champion burger, a chicken-fried sirloin steak, or a Southwestern grilled chicken breast.

STEAKS AND SEAFOOD

The Kangaroo Court (512 River Walk, 210-224-6821; $, □) is a combination oyster bar, restaurant, and pub with something to make anyone happy. The day starts with omelets and pancakes. These are just warm-ups for the daily entrees: Border Fried Quail, Beefsteak Steves, or Shrimp DeMartino, broiled with a garlic crumb crust. The Kangaroo Court is always packed with diners enjoying a meal under the umbrella-shaded tables.

Serious beef lovers should make plans to dine at the **Little Rhein Steakhouse** (231 S. Alamo, 210-225-2111; $$–$$$, □). Located where La Villita meets the River Walk near the Arneson River Theatre, this restaurant offers an excellent selection of fine steaks served on terraces overlooking the river. On less pleasant days, you may choose to dine inside the historic steak house, built in 1847, that witnessed the development of San Antonio under six flags. The stone building also survived the battle of the Alamo only a few blocks away. From the extensive menu here you can choose anything from T-bones to rib eye to Porterhouse steak, all served with Texas caviar, a mixture of black-eyed peas and chopped onion. Reservations are recommended.

TEXAS

Located at street level and above the hustle and bustle of the pedestrian traffic, the **Lone Star Cafe** (237 Losoya, 210-223-9374; $–$$, □) has plenty of good old-fashioned country cooking. Look here for chicken-fried steaks, fried chicken, and some Tex-Mex dishes.

Search for the table umbrellas that look like the Lone Star flag, and you'll have found the **Republic of Texas** (526 River Walk, 210-226-6256; $$, □). This restaurant serves up a little of everything, from fajitas to catfish to burgers, in a building that was once the office of River Walk architect Robert H. H. Hugman. The building still bears his name and the title "Architect" on the former river-level office. Hugman once wrote, "As soon as the river walkway was finished, I opened my office at water level. When I did this, people said, in essence, 'I knew you were a dreamer, but now I know you are also a fool. You'll be drowned like a rat in your own hole.'"

TEX-MEX

Mention **Casa Rio** (430 Commerce, 210-225-9718; $, □) to many locals, and you may hear a snort. Since 1946, this restaurant has been best known as a tourist stop catering to folks eager to try some traditional Tex-Mex right on the banks of the river. But, hey, what's wrong with being popular with the tourist trade? Sure, your fellow diners may say "jal-a-peeno" instead of "hal-a-pen-yo" or (shudder) "fa-ji-tas" instead of "fa-hee-tas," but you'll know better after reading "A Diner's Guide to Mexican Food" (see the Introduction). And there's a real reason behind Casa Rio's long-running popularity—the food. The green chicken and the cheese enchiladas are especially tasty, both served with sides of good ol' cholesterol-laden beans, rice, chips, and tortillas.

There's also plenty of Tex-Mex at **Cafe Ole!** (527 River Walk, 210-223-2939; $, □), located one level up from pedestrian traffic. From the covered porch you can watch the continual conga line of sidewalk activity that parades through this stretch of the walk—all while you've got your hands wrapped around a frozen margarita or a sizzling fajita.

The Original Mexican Restaurant (528 River Walk, 210-224-9951; $–$$, □) dates back to 1899 (although not at this location). Enjoy a seat right on the riverbanks and dine on Tex-Mex fare: enchiladas, fajitas, and tacos washed down with a Mexican *cerveza* or a cold margarita. This restaurant has mariachi musicians on Friday and Saturday nights, so stop by for an authentic San Antonio experience.

One of the most popular River Walk eateries with San Antonio residents is **Rio Rio** (421 E. Commerce, 210-226-8462; $–$$, □). The restaurant has indoor and outdoor dining, and it serves up Tex-Mex favorites from quesadillas to enchiladas.

The newest addition to the Tex-Mex line is the **Texas Tamale Company** (111 W. Crockett St., 210-225-7699; $, ☐), one of the South Bank restaurants still to be opened at press time. This Houston-based Mexican deli specializes in (you guessed it) tamales. Besides the usual, look for beef, chicken, bean, spinach, and cheese. Check out the seasonal gourmet offerings such as quail, venison, and wild boar, as well as special dessert tamales filled with apples and cinnamon.

NIGHTLIFE

Trade in the *sombreros* for tam o' shanters and sing along at **Durty Nelly's Irish Pub** (715 River Walk in the Hilton Palacio Del Rio, 210-222-1400). This bar is modeled after the famous Durty Nelly's Irish Pub in Ireland. Sip Irish ale and munch peanuts, then toss the shells on the floor. This lively joint goes through a ton of goobers every three weeks.

Mention live music and many folks will point you to **Jim Cullum's Landing** (123 Losoya at the Hyatt Regency Hotel, 210-223-7266). Jim Cullum and his jazz band play New Orleans–style Dixieland several nights a week. National Public Radio also tapes shows here (call for dates).

You'll find Dixieland as well as traditional jazz at **Dick's Last Resort** (406 Navarro St., 210-224-0026). This restaurant features many local performers.

The South Bank development, located across the river from Dick's Last Resort, is home to two roaring nightclubs: Fat Tuesdays and Howl at the Moon. **Fat Tuesdays** (111 W. Crockett, 210-212-7886) is a frozen daiquiri bar that bills itself as "a loosely organized street party," bringing the atmosphere of the Big Easy to San Antonio. The proprietors claim to offer the world's largest selection of frozen daiquiris. The newest property, still to be opened at press time, is **Howl at the Moon** (111 W. Crockett, 210-212-4695), a sing-along bar that features dueling pianos. Not for quiet types, the bar is filled with folks singing along to show tunes and classic rock 'n roll songs.

A lot of folks look for a hole-in-the-wall kind of place when they visit a city. That's not easy to find along the River Walk, but the closest you'll come is the **Esquire Bar** (155 E. Commerce St., 210-225-2521). Located on the north bend of the River Walk, just past the floodgates, this joint has been a San Antonio watering hole since 1933. The smoke-filled tavern is dominated by the original bar.

For a laugh, the 400-seat **River Center Comedy Club** (849 E. Commerce in the Rivercenter Mall, 210-229-1420) features both San Antonio's top comics and nationally known comedians. A favorite with locals and visitors alike, reservations are recommended.

ACCOMMODATIONS

On the north side of the horseshoe bend is a hotel with modern conveniences but a historic atmosphere, **La Mansion del Rio** (112 College St., 210-225-2581 or 800-531-7208; $$$, □). This elegant Spanish colonial-style structure began as the St. Mary's Academy in 1854. Eventually the campus grew, was renamed St. Mary's College, and then graduated to St. Mary's University. This location served as the law school until 1966, when the campus was relocated. At that time, the building traded in blackboards for beds, desks for dressers, and started a new life as La Mansion. Today the hotel has 337 rooms and suites, many with private balconies overlooking the River Walk.

Continuing south, you'll reach one of the crown jewels along the River Walk, the **Hyatt Regency San Antonio** (123 Losoya St., 210-222-1234 or 800-233-1234; $$$, □). This hotel is located on the bend in the river and it captures all the excitement of the Paseo del Rio. Whether you enter from the street or the River Walk, you'll admire the soaring atrium filled with palms and the sounds of falling water. Glass elevators whisk guests to the 631 rooms above. The hotel added a segment to the river to divert water through the atrium and into the water gardens beyond. The water garden area now has several small bars and a quieter atmosphere than that found on the River Walk. Follow the steps up the water gardens and you'll soon find yourself facing the Alamo.

Near the Rivercenter Mall, visitors can select from two Marriott hotels. The original property was the **Marriott Riverwalk** (711 E. River Walk, 210-224-4555 or 800-228-9290; $$$, □). Built in 1979, the 500-room hotel is located directly between the mall and the convention center. In keeping with the other upscale properties in this area, a $3.5 million renovation is presently underway.

Just a few steps away, the newest Marriott is the **Marriott Rivercenter** (101 Bowie St., 210-223-1000 or 800-228-9290; $$$, □). This 1,000-room hotel soars from the Rivercenter Mall, looming over the River Walk above any other downtown hotel. The hotel boasts an executive health club with indoor and outdoor pools, a hydrotherapy pool, saunas, and exercise equipment to use if you feel like too many Tex-Mex dinners are slowing you down.

Near the Arneson River Theatre stands the **Hilton Palacio del Rio** (200 S. Alamo St., 210-222-1400 or 800-HILTONS; $$$, ☐). This hotel is a pre-fab, albeit a wonderfully elegant one. The 500-room property was constructed in 202 days for HemisFair. Like giant children's blocks, the rooms (furnishings and all) were assembled off-site and put together here in record time. Today the hotel has a wonderful location, right in the middle of the River Walk action and just a few short steps away from La Villita and HemisFair Plaza.

LA VILLITA

La Villita, the "little village," is nestled on the east bank of the River Walk. Although right off a bustling pedestrian area, La Villita has a much different atmosphere, with an emphasis on history and art. Dating back to the days when the Alamo served as a military outpost, La Villita developed as a temporary village of squatters, people without land title. These tradesmen, camp followers, and Spanish soldiers and their families made their home near the Alamo, living in primitive huts.

For years, La Villita remained a temporary settlement until a disastrous flood in 1821. The San Antonio River rose and demolished much of the west bank, but La Villita with its slightly higher elevation was spared. Locals began to look at the "little village" as the place to be on the river, and soon the temporary huts were replaced with more permanent structures of adobe and stone.

La Villita came to historic prominence during the Texas Revolution when Mexican troopers were defeated after the storming of Bexar. The surrender was signed at the Cos House in the neighborhood. After Texas then became a state, La Villita became a neighborhood of recent immigrants. The look of the neighborhood changed from Spanish adobe to European-style limestone blocks.

Within 50 years, though, La Villita hit bottom, reduced to a collection of boarding houses and bathhouses on the river's edge. Water was hauled from the river and sold for a quarter a barrel. The region became a virtual slum. It remained one of the worst areas in the city until 1939. As the city turned its attention to the river, planners realized that La Villita was long due a renovation. The National Youth Administration and the city began an extensive program of renovation and re-creation. Today this is a National Historic District, filled with structures that recall Texas's early days.

The historic buildings here now house artisans and craftsmen at work on everything from fine hand-blown glass to woven shawls. You'll find Latin American imports, from tin art to Indian rugs, sold alongside the creations of San Antonio artists. This artists' community nestles between San Antonio's tallest structure and the age-old river. One square block in size, it has retained an air of separateness from the River Walk, a place for people to shop for fine souvenirs in a collection of buildings whose styles hark back to the days of Old San Antonio.

For information on La Villita happenings, call (210) 207-8610. For brochures and information on group tours, stop by the **Best of Texas Tours** (303 S. Alamo, 210-225-2378), located next to the Guadalajara Grill.

ATTRACTIONS

Start your visit at the **La Villita Tourist Information Center** for a free copy of "A Walking Tour of La Villita." This brochure will lead you to the Florian House (built for $660 in 1854 for a Polish immigrant), to the old St. Philip's College, and to the Tejada house, one of the oldest structures in La Villita.

The **Cos House** (418 Villita St.) is called by some the birthplace of Texas independence. Here the articles of capitulation were signed in December 9, 1835, relinquishing Mexico's claim to all lands north of the Rio Grande. When General Cos returned to Mexico City and told Santa Anna of the surrender, Santa Anna swore revenge and headed his troops for the Alamo. Today the home is not open for tours.

Another historic site is the **Little Church at La Villita** (210-226-3593). The cornerstone was laid March 2, 1879, and since then the structure has served many denominations. Services are held Sundays at 11 a.m. and 6 p.m., and the rest of the week it's not uncommon to see a wedding in this presently nondenominational church.

Just a few steps away, the **Glassblowing Museum** (210-226-3542, small admission fee) is housed in a glassblower's shop. Five hundred items and exhibits on glassblowing sit on display.

SHOPPING

There's no doubt that La Villita, for all its historic interest, is best known as a "shop 'til you drop" kind of place. Visitors and locals alike enjoy browsing for one-of-a-kind items with a Southwestern flair.

An artists' cooperative called **Galleria II** (210-227-0527) is housed in a Victorian building that dates back to 1873. You'll see artists at work creating pottery, stained glass, and watercolor paintings. Located next to the Little Church, the **River Art Group Gallery** (210-226-8752) represents the work of 500 artists and craftsmen. The River Art Group was founded in 1947, making it the city's oldest art group. Today its members sponsor the annual River Art Show in October and display their works year-round in the gallery, which is open daily. If you're looking for a watercolor of the Paseo del Rio, this is the place. Fireplace pokers, branding irons, foot scrapers, and bootjacks are other popular purchases.

If crafts are on your list, stop by **Villita Stained Glass** (210-223-4480) or the **Village Gallery** (210-226-0404); the latter features hand-blown glass plus stoneware and pottery. You'll find Texas crafts, gourmet foods, clothing, and cookbooks at **Country Charm** (210-223-4199).

Hand-woven clothing, placemats, rugs, and more are the specialties of the **Village Weavers** (210-222-0776). This shop handles the work of artists from both San Antonio and many Latin American countries. Blankets, skirts, sweaters, and other textiles abound in this interesting shop.

Two La Villita shops feature Latin American collectibles. **Angelita's** (210-224-8362) is the oldest import boutique in the city, offering a mixture of clothing and jewelry from Mexico, Guatemala, and several Central America countries. The shop is housed in an adobe building that dates back to the mid-1800s (watch out for the low doorway!). Nearby, **Casa Manos Alegres** (210-224-5107) features Latin American folk art, from tin art to *milagros* (miracle charms) to nativity sets.

DINING

La Villita and the River Walk share the **Little Rhein Steakhouse** (231 S. Alamo, 210-225-2111; $$,☐). The Otto Bombach House and Store is now the kitchen and indoor seating area for this popular restaurant. The menu here tempts with everything from T-bone to Porterhouse. During nice weather, most diners opt for outdoor dining on terraces perched over the River Walk. Reservations are recommended.

The most elegant and pricey restaurant at La Villita, and indeed in the city, is **The Fig Tree** (515 Paseo De La Villita, 210-224-1976; $$$, ☐), where Continental cuisine is the order of the day. The *prix fixe* menu features beef Wellington, lobster, and rack of lamb, as well as buffalo rib eye, venison and antelope tenderloins, and quail. This restaurant is open for dinner only, and reservations are recommended.

Don't worry about reservations or blowing your entire vacation budget at the **Guadalajara Grill** (301 S. Alamo St., 210-222-1992; $, ☐). Start off with a plate of nachos and follow up with fajitas, red snapper, mole poblano, grilled chicken breast with mole sauce, or even catfish. There's seating inside this relaxed restaurant and along the sidewalk as well.

ACCOMMODATIONS

La Villita, which packs a lot into one city block, does not offer hotel or bed-and-breakfast accommodations. You will find several excellent choices within easy walking distance, however.

The **Hilton Palacio del Rio** (see the "River Walk" chapter) is located next to the Arneson River Theatre, the River Walk entrance to La Villita.

Across Nueva Street, the **Fairmount Hotel** provides luxurious accommodations, as does the **Plaza Hotel** just one block beyond. (See the "HemisFair" chapter for details on these two properties.)

If you're especially interested in the historic buildings at La Villita, consider a stay in one of the King William district's (see that chapter) many B & Bs. The stately homes in this neighborhood were built by the businessmen of early San Antonio.

ALAMO PLAZA

Mention "San Antonio de Valero" and only the most dedicated history buffs know that you're referring to the Alamo. Although many tourists who walk through the corridors of the structure never realize it, the Alamo is just a nickname for the mission.

The name comes from military occupation. The mission was abandoned in 1793 and the buildings began to fall to ruin. Troops from San Jose y Santiago del Alamo Parras in northern Mexico converted the building to a fort in 1801, and it took the name of that troop. Since that moniker was a real mouthful, the nickname was later shortened to simply "El Alamo." And just what is the English translation of Alamo? "Cottonwood."

Alamo Plaza is at one time historic and hysterical, the ultimate shrine to Texas history alongside shrines to the Texas tourist. This one-block area is the home of the Alamo, the mission that represents the fight for freedom and the spirit of Texas. It's a place where tones are hushed and respectful, a destination to which every true Texan makes a pilgrimage at least once in his or her life. In juxtaposition, Alamo Plaza is also the home of the heart of the city's most tourist-oriented businesses: souvenir stands, a wax museum, and a bounty of tour companies. But somehow, this all works together to give visitors the feeling of visiting a site worthy of both solemnity and souvenirs.

The story of the Alamo is a tale taught to every young Texan: the story of fewer than 200 brave volunteers who faced nearly 10 times as many Mexican troops in a battle whose outcome was already determined. To further the cause of Texas independence, they gave their lives but won a place in the history of the Lone Star State.

The battle of the Alamo was preceded by battles in Gonzales, Goliad, and in San Antonio itself. Mexican troops led by General Cos had taken refuge in the Alamo and surrendered in early December. The surrender had angered Santa Anna. He vowed to get rid of the Anglos and also to punish the Tejanos, the Mexicans living in Texas that had taken part in the battle.

After the surrender, the Texas army floundered without a leader for several months, and its numbers dwindled. Simultaneously, Santa Anna was rallying his troops for the long journey from Mexico City to San Antonio.

Texas troops still occupied the Alamo, joined by volunteers such as Davy Crockett. The troops felt they had time before Santa Anna would arrive, but they were wrong. Santa Anna's advance troops first arrived in San Antonio on February 23. The revolutionaries scrambled inside the protective walls of the mission, bringing in a sufficient amount of cattle and supplies that commander William Travis felt could sustain them until help arrived.

Travis quickly made the appeal for more troops, knowing that the brunt of Santa Anna's army was only days away. The help so desperately needed did not arrive, and on March 3 Travis allegedly drew a line in the earth with his sword. All men who wanted to stay and defend the Alamo crossed the line—exhibiting their dedication to independence even at the cost of battling an enemy that vastly outnumbered them. Only one man did not cross the line.

The battle began with bombardments from Mexican cannons, but the real surge took place at about 5:30 the morning of March 6. Perhaps as many as 1,800 Mexican soldiers stormed the mission, fighting first with guns and finally hand to hand as they progressed up the walls. By 7 a.m., the battle was over. All the Texas revolutionaries died or were executed, but Santa Anna's troops permitted several women and a slave of William Travis's to live. The most famous survivors were Suzanna Dickinson and her daughter Angelina, the family of an Alamo officer. They were left to spread the word of the Alamo defeat. And spread the word they did. "Remember the Alamo" was the battle cry in the months to come, when finally the Texans defeated Santa Anna at the Battle of San Jacinto. Texas then became an independent republic.

ATTRACTIONS

If you visit only one San Antonio attraction, make it the **Alamo** (300 Alamo Plaza, 210-225-1391; free). The most famous site in Texas, this mission is now a symbol of the fight for freedom in the battle for independence from Mexico. It's often referred to as the "cradle of Texas liberty," and even today talk is hushed here, men remove their hats, and photography is prohibited. It stands as a reminder of the Spanish colonization of this area and of the bloody battle that was fought so valiantly.

Built as San Antonio de Valero, the Alamo was originally a large compound. Today all that remains of the mission is the original church and the Long Barracks. When you enter the Alamo, you'll be struck by the quietness of the structure. It retains a chapel-like atmosphere in spite of the hundreds of thousands of visitors who tour the park annually. Most first-time visitors budget two or three hours for a look at the chapel and its displays, the barracks, and the film about the story of the historic battle.

The Alamo operates under the care of the Daughters of the Alamo, a conservation group that protects the mission and guards it, many say, as fiercely as the Texian troops did a century and a half ago. (The "Texians" were the citizens of Texas during Mexican reign; residents became "Texans" after the revolution.)

Directly in front of the Alamo stands the **Alamo Cenotaph,** a monument to the men who lost their lives in the battle. The marble monument, designed by Italian-born and Texas-adopted sculptor Pompeo Coppini, includes all the names of the Alamo defenders. Vehicles are no longer permitted in this area, a gesture of respect for the Indians buried in a cemetery found in front of the chapel.

There are two visitors centers in this area: the **Visitors Information Center** (317 Alamo Plaza, 210-299-8155), operated by the San Antonio Convention and Visitors Bureau, and the **Alamo Visitor Center** (216 Alamo Plaza, 210-225-8587). The Visitors Information Center, directly across from the Alamo, provides brochures and maps, and the staff can help with travel questions. The Alamo Visitors Center provides brochures on area attractions and sells tickets for the IMAX, San Antonio City Tours, the Texas Trolley, the riverboat rides, Sea World of Texas, and Fiesta Texas.

The newest attraction in Alamo Plaza is **The Texas Adventure** (307 Alamo Plaza, 210-227-8224; admission fee). The unique theater calls itself the world's first "Encountarium F-X Theatre," using state of the art technology to move beyond traditional movie techniques to tell this classic tale. Here you can see a version of the fall of the Alamo played out with animatronics and holographic figures. Guests are first ushered into a room for a six-minute preshow using excellent dioramas to explain the events that led up to the famous battle. Next, visitors take a seat on benches where the story comes to life with holographic versions of Crockett, Travis, and Bowie. The presentation lasts 24 minutes, and it's suitable for anyone except very young children. (When Jim Bowie "appeared" out of thin air, a young child seated near us let loose a scream the likes of which may not have been heard in these parts since the battle itself.)

Just down the street, the **Plaza Theatre of Wax** (301 Alamo Plaza, 210-224-9299; admission fee) is a museum depicting the famous, from Jesus to John Wayne. The sculptures are well done and many are displayed in elaborate sets featuring movie scenes.

HIDDEN TREASURES:
THE COWBOY MUSEUM AND GALLERY

If you walk down Alamo Plaza, you might notice Jack Glover before you see the Cowboy Museum. Even in the varied crowd found milling around the Alamo, he's a hard one to miss. Clad in chaps, vest, and what surely must be a 10-gallon hat (complete with badge), Glover looks like he just stepped out of the 19th century. This Western artist is one of three owners of the Cowboy Museum, showcasing the culture of the Texas cowboy and Old San Antone. It's a bawdy history, filled with brothels, brawls, and barbed wire disputes. Much of the collection has been owned by Glover for decades, and he's eager to tell you the story behind any of the interesting pieces.

You'll enter the museum through swinging saloon doors and step back to the days of a much wilder San Antonio. The first exhibit is a longhorn steer over 125 years old. The regal animal has survived so long because his hide is pickled, not tanned. This longhorn is representative of the cattle business that was so important to Texas and to the brave men who took on the dangerous job of driving the four-legged commodity to the stockyards.

Barbed wire was very controversial in the 19th century, so much in fact that it's still illegal in Texas to carry a pair of wire-cutters in your back pocket! An extensive collection displays numerous varieties of barbed wire, from plain styles with a double barb to some with star-shaped prongs.

You'll also see many sorts of branding irons on display. Brands were introduced to Texas by the Spaniards. In case you ever wondered how to tell if a brand is "crazy" or "lazy," the "crazy" variety is one where the letter is turned left horizontally. To make a "lazy" brand, turn the letter to the right until it lies horizontally.

Indians played a large part in the settling of Texas, and the most famous in the area was Chief Quannah Parker. You'll see his peyote box on display, which once held hallucinogenic peyote used for ceremonial purposes. The exhibit also contains an English-made brush, comb, and mirror set owned by Parker's favorite wife, Topai. The story goes that when an Indian agent learned that Parker had seven wives, he told the chief he should

Continued

only have one. Quannah Parker allegedly replied, "Okay, good idea—*you* tell 'em."

The neighboring Sioux exhibit is one of the museum's most unusual, containing, for example, a necklace made from human finger and hand bones. You'll also see displays of Native American dress, and an explanation of the importance of color in the attire. White signified snow or winter, the time when braves went on the warpath; blue, which was boiled out of Cavalry uniforms and trade blankets, could signify anything from lakes to sky to the wind.

Much of the museum is devoted to the Wild West days of Old San Antone. In one fascinating part of the museum, you can walk on the actual boardwalks used in the older part of the city. They were ripped up and salvaged from the present HemisFair site in 1968, and today they are laid out with store facades to represent the early days of the city. Walk on the planks and have a look inside the windows of the Wild West fronts, from the undertaker's to the general store to the jail house.

Of course, no frontier town would be complete without its brothel, and San Antonio had its own. You'll see a white wicker-sided carriage here, the "Carriage of the Soiled Dove," which was used to parade the bawdy house's newest girl up Houston Street, around Alamo Plaza, and down Commerce Street.

Other wagons at the museum include a doctor's buggy and a brewery wagon. The latter was actually used until 1910 to carry beer to the many saloons in town.

Alamo visitors will appreciate the "Heroes of the Lone Star" exhibits on the fateful battle. A note to parents: The Theater of Horrors is especially scary for young (and even not-so-young) children. However, this attraction is accessible only by entering a well-marked door at the bottom of a staircase, so you can easily skip the stairs and bypass the creepy exhibits without even a peek.

The wax museum is housed in the same building as **Ripley's Believe It or Not!** and combination tickets to both attractions are available. Ripley's displays an assortment of over 500 oddities ranging from miniatures to freaks of nature. Even if you don't go in, have a look at the robotic dinosaur at the entrance.

On a more historic note, the **Cowboy Museum** (209 Alamo Plaza, 210-229-1257; admission fee) recalls the role that cowboys have played in the state's history.

SHOPPING

The Menger Hotel (204 Alamo Plaza) is home to an assortment of small shops that offer everything from posters to fine art and T-shirts to antiques. One unique store is **Kings X** (210-226-7000), a collection of miniature toy soldiers representing warriors from medieval times to World War II. There are even tiny fighting men from the Battle of the Alamo available here.

Next door, **J. Adelman Antiques and Art** (210-225-5914) offers estate jewelry, crystal, china, and antique art in an elegant setting. The neighboring **Posters on the Plaza** (210-227-0808) stocks an extensive collection of Southwestern and Latin American folk art, jewelry, and, of course, posters. **San Antonio Style** (210-223-9979) sells things Texan, from specialty foods to T-shirts, and the **Silver Spur** (210-224-7669) will outfit you like a city cowboy or cowgirl.

Across the street, you'll find **Woolworth** (210-227-3932). Since 1912 this dime store has supplied Alamo visitors with the necessary souvenirs: coonskin caps, pop pistols, and images of the Alamo on everything from thimbles to spoon rests. This two-story emporium is a very popular stop with the little folks in the family.

Just down the street, **Booksmiths** (209 Alamo Plaza, 210-271-9177 or 800-688-3927) has one of the area's best collections of regional guides, cookbooks, Texas history tomes, and literary works from state writers. **The Red Balloon** (210-271-9461 or 800-688-3927), located in the same complex, is a children's bookstore that stocks Caldecott and Newberry award winners and related merchandise for kids.

DINING

If you're looking for Texas barbecue, head to **Uncle Hoppy's Bar-B-Cue** (329 Alamo Plaza, 210-227-2422; $–$$, □). The slogan here is "If it ain't Uncle Hoppy's, it's pot roast." Well, we don't know about that, but you can find plenty of good old-fashioned 'cue here: brisket, chicken, turkey, sausage, and pork ribs served with sides of potato salad, coleslaw, pintos, or candied yams.

NIGHTLIFE

You might feel as if you've stepped into an English pub at the **Menger Bar** (204 Alamo St., 210-223-4361). There's a jolly good reason—the establishment is a replica of London's House of Lords Pub. Paneled in dark woods, this historic bar was built in 1887 and is best known as the place where Teddy Roosevelt recruited his Rough Riders in 1898.

ACCOMMODATIONS

The **Menger Hotel** (204 Alamo St., 210-223-4361; $$, □) is located just next door to the Alamo. This historic hotel was built in 1859 and has remained a popular stop ever since. Some of its most famous guests include Civil War generals Robert E. Lee and William Sherman, Mount Rushmore sculptor Gutzon Borglum (who had a studio at the hotel), playwright Oscar Wilde, and author William Sydney Porter (O. Henry), who mentioned the hotel in several of his short stories. Today the Menger has been restored to its Victorian splendor. The three-story lobby features Corinthian columns, a leaded skylight, and much of the original furniture. Guests can stay in Victorian accommodations or newer rooms in the addition, and have access to a complete spa. The lobby is adjacent to a tropical garden (once the home of several alligators) and shopping. Directly across the street are the stores of Blum Street and the Rivercenter Mall (see the "River Walk" chapter for details on those.)

On the north side of the Alamo stands the **Ramada Emily Morgan** (705 E. Houston, 210-225-8486 or 800-824-6674; $-$$, □). This hotel is named for the woman known in legend and song as "The Yellow Rose of Texas." General Santa Anna was enamored with Emily Morgan, a mulatto slave who acted as a spy for the Texas army. Thanks in part to her efforts, Sam Houston's troops defeated Santa Anna's men at San Jacinto on April 21, 1836, winning the Texas Revolution. The rooms here overlook the Alamo courtyard or Alamo Plaza, and all have Jacuzzis.

Just beyond Alamo Plaza stands the **Crockett Hotel** (320 Bonham, 210-225-6500 or 800-292-1050; $$-$$$, □), situated on grounds that were once part of the Alamo battlefield. In fact, Davy Crockett was said to have defended the southeast palisade, and the hotel is named in his honor. The original mercantile store that stood at this site was sold to the International Order of Odd Fellows, who built a lodge and hotel here in 1909. Today the 202-room hotel has been faithfully restored to its turn-of-the-century grandeur. Guests can enjoy a rooftop hot tub and sun deck or a landscaped pool with its own waterfall.

Also downtown but not actually on Alamo Plaza you'll find two distinct hotels that exude the elegance of old San Antonio: the **St. Anthony** (300 E. Travis, 210-227-4392; $$, ☐) and the **Sheraton Gunter** (205 E. Houston, 210-227-3241; $$, ☐).

KING WILLIAM
HISTORIC DISTRICT

If there's a preferred address in San Antonio, it's most likely in the King William Historic District. Just a stone's throw south of the River Walk, this neighborhood boasts elegant homes, stately shade trees, and an atmosphere of grace and gentility.

Its status as a superior neighborhood goes back to the mid-1800s, when this district was populated by the Alamo City's most successful businessmen and their families. Many of these frontier citizens were German immigrants with names like Guenther, Wulff, and Heusinger. With their wealth gained in merchandising and investing, they set about building the most lavish homes in the city, most in the grand Victorian style.

One of the most opulent of these residences was the Steves Homestead, positioned right on the banks of the river. Besides a natatorium and a carriage house, the home also boasted the finest furnishings and detail work of its era. Today it's open for public tours (see "Attractions" in this chapter), as is the Guenther House next to Pioneer Flour Mills. The old mill still churns out some of the best flour gravy mix found on grocery shelves, along with cornbread, pancake, and similar mixes.

Other homes in King William are privately owned, but residents are accustomed to tour buses and pedestrians sight-seeing in the area. You can enjoy a self-guided tour by picking up a brochure ("King William Area—A Walking Tour") in front of the San Antonio Conservation Society headquarters in the Anton Wulff House (107 King William St., 210-224-6163) or at a visitors center in town. The walk takes you past over three dozen stately homes.

Organized home tours are conducted annually on the Saturday following Thanksgiving. For tour information, write the King William Association, 1032 S. Alamo St., San Antonio, TX 78210, or call 210-227-8786.

ATTRACTIONS

On a walk or a driving tour of King William, you may wonder just what the inside of these mansions is like. Satisfy your curiosity with a tour of the **Steves Homestead** (509 King William St., 210-

225-5924; admission fee). Once the home of German immigrant Edward Steves, founder of Steves Lumber Company, today the grand house is owned by the San Antonio Conservation Society.

Another outstanding residence open to the public is the **Guenther House** (205 E. Guenther, 210-227-1061; free). Built in 1860, this was the home of Carl Hilmar Guenther, founder of Pioneer Flour Mills. With its crystal chandelier, gold leaf mirrors, and piano from Stuttgart, Germany, the parlor offers a lovely glimpse of the elegance once enjoyed by the Guenther family. The home's library is now a **museum,** displaying pieces used by Pioneer Flour throughout the years, from Dresden china anniversary plates to cookie cutters and family photos. The **San Antonio River Mill Store** is housed in the former music room and bedroom, and visitors can purchase stoneware, baking accessories, and gift items here. Finally, the **Guenther House Restaurant,** decorated in the Art Nouveau style, serves breakfast, lunch, and Sunday brunch.

The McDaniel Carriage House, built in 1896, is now the home of the **San Antonio Art League** (130 King William St., 210-223-1140; free). Have a look at changing exhibits featuring various types of art, from members' current works to pieces from previous decades. Open Tuesday through Saturday.

SHOPPING

If you're looking for contemporary art, head to the **Blue Star Arts Complex** (1400 S. Alamo, 210-227-6960). Located on the banks of the river, the complex is a stop on the King William/Blue Star trolley line. The main feature is the 11,000-square-foot **Contemporary Art Museum,** operated by the artists. Other galleries feature folk art, experimental media, ceramics, and furniture. The **Milagros Contemporary Art Gallery** displays contemporary art from Latin American, European, and American artists.

DINING

When stomachs start to growl in your group, take a quick trip south of the border at **Rosario's** (1014 S. Alamo, 210-223-1806; $$, ▢). This cafe and cantina is popular with the arts community in King William, but it's equally popular for its specialties: tortilla soup, *enchiladas de mole, chiles rellenos,* and *carne de puerco cascabel* (pork tips in red chile sauce).

Milder fare is the order of the day at the **Guenther House Restaurant** (205 E. Guenther St., 210-227-1061; $, □). This restaurant in the former home of Carl Guenther, founder of Pioneer Flour, features (not too surprisingly) plenty of biscuits and gravy, sweet cream waffles, and pancakes. After a morning of looking at King William's elegant homes, enjoy a light lunch of salad, sandwich, or soup.

ACCOMMODATIONS

Many of King William's residents have decided to convert their homes into bed-and-breakfast accommodations. These offer an elegant way to enjoy a quiet stay just a short stroll from the downtown River Walk areas, all the while enjoying a look at San Antonio's most opulent historic homes.

The **Beckmann Inn and Carriage House** (222 E. Guenther St., 210-229-1449 or 800-945-1449; $$, □) dates back to 1886 when it was built for the daughter of the Guenther flour mill family. Originally this home's address was on Madison Street, but in 1913 the owners decided to extend the front porch around the house on the Guenther Street side. They wanted a new street address, one not shared by the notorious brothel also located on Madison Street at the time! Today this Victorian inn has four guest rooms, each with private baths, and also an adjacent carriage house with a private entrance. Owners Betty Jo and Don Schwartz love vacationers. Natives of Illinois, the couple fell in love with San Antonio during a visit for the 1968 World HemisFair and finally moved to the city just a few years ago.

One of the most elegant bed-and-breakfast accommodations in the city is the **Ogé House** (209 Washington, 210-223-2353; $$, □). This 1857 three-story plantation-style home has king and queen rooms filled with antiques. Located directly on the Paseo del Rio, this lovely spot is just minutes away from restaurants and shopping.

Another popular King William bed-and-breakfast is **A Yellow Rose of Texas** (229 Madison, 210-229-9903 or 800-950-9903; $–$$, □). The 1878 home has undergone a major renovation and now provides an elegant Victorian atmosphere in five double rooms with private baths and cable TV.

Rustic elegance is the theme of the **Riverwalk Inn** (329 Old Guilbeau Rd., 210-212-8300 or 800-254-4440; $–$$, □). This unique bed-and-breakfast utilizes five two-story log homes, each built circa 1840. These structures were combined to form the two buildings that house this 11-room inn, which is located directly on the River Walk. Decorated with country antiques, each room has a fireplace, a private bath, cable TV, a refrigerator, and a phone with voice mail.

Other popular bed-and-breakfasts include the **Gatlin Guesthouse** (123 Cedar St., 800-317-7143; $, ☐), the **Royal Swan** (236 Madison, 210-223-3776; $–$$, ☐), and the **River Haus Bed and Breakfast** (107 Woodward, 210-226-2524; $, ☐).

HEMISFAIR PLAZA

In 1968, the eyes of the world turned to San Antonio. This was the site of HemisFair '68, a world's fair that brought the citizens of the globe to the Alamo City.

Five years of construction went into the fairgrounds, creating new landmarks such as the soaring Tower of the Americas and restoring 19th-century structures as well. When all was done, the fairgrounds gave visitors a fascinating look at the new and the old, from computer-based instructional systems (one of the first glimpses of this modern tool) to the Flying Indians of Papantla, a recreation of an Aztec ritual whereby dancers held by ropes around their waists swung around a 114-foot tall pole. Visitors to Hemis-Fair were transported by the Skyride (a mini monorail) or aboard a lagoon cruise. They dined on the food of the world, from Mexican *buñelos* to Belgian waffles, and shopped for souvenirs from the many countries represented.

Today most of the activity here surrounds the Tower of the Americas, the nearby water gardens, and the museums. Other buildings remain, but many are closed. Plans are underway to transform a section of the area into the German Heritage Park, with a coffee house, *biergarten,* health spa, and shops.

ATTRACTIONS

No matter from which direction you approach San Antonio, you'll see the **Tower of the Americas** (210-299-8615; admission fee) looming over the skyline. This symbol of the 1968 World Hemis-Fair remains a landmark for downtown San Antonio. The Tower soars 750 feet from the base to the top of the antennae, but visitors view the city from the observation deck at 579 feet. Close to three decades after its construction, this is still one of the tallest free-standing structures in the Western hemisphere—87 feet taller than the Seattle Space Needle and 67 feet higher than the Washington Monument.

Since its construction, the Tower and its grounds have undergone many changes. In April 1988, HemisFair Park was rededicated after a $12 million renovation of the grounds. In March 1990, a $1.2 million restoration was completed on the Tower itself. Today you can enjoy a one-minute elevator ride traveling seven miles per hour to the observation deck, where high-powered telescopes provide a bird's-eye view of the city's sights. Eight panoramic photo panels help locate major attractions. Both enclosed and open-air observation decks are open, and an evening visit is especially breathtaking. The deck is open nightly until 11 p.m.

Nearby, the **Institute of Texan Cultures** (801 S. Bowie, 210-558-2300; free) is one of the best museums in town. Operated by the University of Texas, this museum explores the 30-plus ethnic cultures that settled Texas. Don't miss the dome slide show (offered four times daily) for a look at the many faces of the Lone Star State. Children especially love this place. Most days you'll find costumed docents throughout the museum, ready to educate visitors about the role of a chuck wagon cook on a cattle drive or the rigors of life as a frontier woman. Open Tuesday through Sunday, many hands-on displays keep young visitors interested and full of questions.

For more on the Mexican heritage that is so much a part of San Antonio, visit the **Mexican Cultural Institute** (600 HemisFair Plaza, 210-227-0123; free). This museum (open Tuesday through Sunday) focuses on the culture of Latin America with exhibits of contemporary works by Mexican and South American artists.

The newest (and largest) attraction in downtown San Antonio is the massive **Alamodome** (100 Montana St., 210-207-3652 for tour information; admission fee). This 65,000-seat, $186.3-million dome is a busy place. Home of the San Antonio Spurs basketball team, the site hosts concerts, trade shows and conventions, and various sporting events as well. You also can take a tour for a behind-the-scenes look; the Alamodome is the only place in North America with two permanent Olympic-sized ice rinks under the same roof, and it's the home of the world's largest single unit of retractable seats.

DINING

For the best view of the city, head up the Tower of the Americas to the **Tower Restaurant** (210-223-3101; $$, □), open for lunch and dinner daily. Steak and seafood are the specialties of the house, all enjoyed in a revolving atmosphere (the restaurant makes one complete revolution per hour). Above the eating area, the Cloud Room has a full bar and dance floor.

The neighboring Plaza San Antonio Hotel is home to the **Anaqua Grill** (555 S. Alamo St., 210-229-1000; $$$, □). Located just off the lobby, this sunny restaurant has indoor and outdoor seating (where you may be joined by Chinese pheasants that roam the grounds). The menu features New American cuisine, ranging from Mediterranean-influenced pastas to Tex-Mex selections.

The most highly acclaimed restaurant in this area (and one of the most praised in San Antonio) is **Polo's at the Fairmount** (401 S. Alamo St., 800-642-3363; $$–$$$, □). *Esquire* magazine called this eatery "one of the most innovative in the country" and *The New York Times* lauded it as "the chicest in San Antonio." But judge for yourself at breakfast, lunch, or dinner. Give the seafood pizza a try, or, if you're in a Texas mood, nibble on the venison sausage pizza. The dinner menu takes on an international flair with choices such as New Zealand lamb, grilled Norwegian salmon, and good ol' barbecued quail in raspberry chipotle sauce.

ACCOMMODATIONS

Just across the street from HemisFair Park stands the **Plaza San Antonio Hotel** (555 S. Alamo, 800-421-1172; $$, □), boasting the most beautiful grounds of the downtown hotels—six acres shaded by massive oaks and pecans. The hotel has 252 guest rooms, each with a private balcony. Guests have use of a health club, a heated outdoor pool and spa, lighted tennis courts, lawn croquet facilities, bicycles for touring, walking and jogging maps, and complimentary transportation downtown on weekdays.

A unique feature of this elegant resort is the annexation of historic buildings that add style and atmosphere. Four 19th-century structures, each listed on the National Register of Historic Places, are located directly behind the hotel. The Diaz House, now used for meetings and receptions, was built around 1840. Some have pointed out the similarity of the stonework in the Diaz House and that in the outer wall of the Alamo. The health club is housed in an 1850s structure that typifies the German style so popular in San Antonio during that period. Yet another house, now a private dining room, was saved as an example of a Victorian cottage.

But the best known of the hotel's historic structures is the German-English School. Located next to the tennis courts, this two-story building was originally built to teach the children of the German businessmen who lived in the affluent King William neighborhood. Now the hotel conference center, the school came to national attention in 1992 when U.S. President Bush, Mexican President Salinas, and Canadian Prime Minister Mulroney met here for the initializing ceremony of the North American Free Trade Agreement.

Next door to the Plaza stands the **Fairmount Hotel** (401 S. Alamo, 210-224-8800 or 800-642-3363; $$$, □), calling itself "San Antonio's Little Jewel." This 37-room property pampers its guests with personal attention and style amid turn-of-the-century elegance. In 1986 the hotel earned a place in the *Guinness Book of World Records* when the 3.2-million-pound structure became the heaviest building ever moved. The move took six days, relocating the three-story hotel just across the street from both HemisFair Plaza and La Villita. In excavating the basement at its new home, artifacts from the battle of the Alamo were found. Today the site is a State Archaeological Landmark.

After the relocation, the property received an extensive renovation, leaving the guest rooms transformed by soft pastel tones, marble baths, canopy beds, and endless amenities.

MISSION TRAIL

Mention the missions, and most people think you're referring to the Alamo. But San Antonio is home to four other Spanish missions from the same period, each giving visitors a sense of both the Franciscan missionaries and the Indians who made the sites their home.

Texas at one time hosted 38 missions, all built by the Spanish, that served to convert the Indians to Catholicism and to enforce the claim of Spain to the area in the face of rival European powers, especially France. The San Antonio missions all sprang up near the river, which supplied water for crop irrigation. The water was channeled to the missions by means of an *acequia,* or irrigation ditch.

Visitors to the Alamo cannot appreciate the area typically covered by these compounds. When visiting the four structures along the Mission Trail, however, you'll see the size and scope of these communities, which usually included a chapel, Indian living quarters, a smithy, a granary to store crops, and farmland. The missions operated as independent communities presided over by Franciscan friars.

The first San Antonio mission, San Antonio de Valero or the Alamo, was built to serve as a way station between missions in East Texas and those along the Rio Grande. The East Texas establishments proved unsuccessful, however, due to changing policy toward the French in Louisiana and widespread epidemics that resulted from settling in the swampy woodlands. In 1731, three missions were relocated to San Antonio, forming one of the densest concentration of Spanish missions in the New World.

The Indians who lived in the missions were Coahuiltecans, hunter-gatherers from South Texas and northeastern Mexico. Because European diseases had taken their toll on the native population and nomadic tribes were moving in on their lands, the Indians allowed themselves to be recruited by the friars. By the late 1700s, the missions had become secularized due to the full adaptation of the remaining Indians to Spanish culture and the Catholic faith. Many of the mission buildings began to fall to ruin as a result of instability resulting from the breakdown of Spanish rule.

In the 1920s the citizens of San Antonio, through the San Antonio Conservation Society, began to preserve the deteriorating structures. In 1978 the San Antonio Missions National Historic Park was established, protecting and operating the four sites. The cooperative effort between the Park Service, the San Antonio Conservation Society, and the State of Texas was expanded by a cooperative agreement with the Archdiocese of San Antonio. As a result, the missions continue as active churches.

Today the missions are each open to the public free of charge, and donations are welcome. The drive along the mission trail is somewhat hard to follow (even the National Park Service brochure warns that "the route that connects the four missions can be confusing for visitors"). The way is marked with brown park signs, but it twists and turns between residential neighborhoods and parks. Further, during heavy rains, two low-water crossings are closed, necessitating an alternate route. The free brochure from the National Park Service outlines both the traditional Mission Trail as well as other routes to take during inclement weather.

When planning your visit, remember that these are active parish churches (unlike the Alamo). Services are conducted every Sunday, and respectful visitors are welcome. Mission San José has a Mariachi Mass every Sunday at noon; it is very popular with visitors.

ATTRACTIONS

Most tours of the Mission Trail start at the Alamo, and it's only a few miles south to the first mission. From the Alamo, head south on Broadway, one block west of North Alamo Street (a one-way northbound avenue). Broadway becomes Alamo Street when it crosses Commerce Street. Continue south on Alamo Street to the intersection of South St. Mary's Street. Turn left (south) and continue to the intersection of Mission Road. Here you'll see a Park Service sign for the Mission Trail. Turn right.

Just to the right you'll see the intersection of Lone Star Boulevard. This is the turn for visitors on a completely different mission—that of touring **Lone Star Brewery** (600 Lone Star Blvd., 210-270-9467; admission fee). In 1881 the Buckhorn Saloon opened as a Texan watering hole. Soon hunters and trappers were stopping by, and, eager for a cold brew, they traded in furs and horns. Owner Albert Friedrich collected the horns, some which his father made into horn chairs. Today you can see trophies on guided tours through the Buckhorn Hall of Fins (marine trophies and fishing lures), the Buckhorn Hall of Feathers (mounted birds), and Buckhorn Hall of Horns (heads, hides, and horns that were often exchanged at the bar for a drink).

Not all exhibits here are stuffed—some are wax. The Hall of Texas History Wax Museum features a recreation of the Battle of the Alamo and other important Texas events.

Another brewery attraction is the O. Henry home, still furnished with the writer's personal effects. The adobe building was originally located on South Presa, but William Sydney Porter (a.k.a. O. Henry) did have a connection to the Lone Star Brewery, albeit through a beer mug filled frequently at the Buckhorn Saloon.

After a visit to the brewery, or if you decide to save that for another day, return to Mission Road and continue south. Along the way you'll pass the **Yturri-Edmunds House and Mill** (257 Yellowstone at Mission Trail, 210-224-6163; free). When the missions were secularized, this land formerly belonged to Mission Concepción. It was granted to Manuel Yturri-Castillo, and he built an adobe home here. Today you can tour the residence as well as the shady grounds.

Continue on Mission Road beneath the I-10 overpass and soon you'll arrive at **Mission Concepción** (807 Mission Rd., 210-229-5732). This site is tucked into a residential neighborhood, a quiet place far different from the bustling Alamo area. Concepción (pronounced "con-cep-see-OWN") was moved here in 1731 from East Texas. Its full name is a mouthful: Mission of Nuestra Señora de la Purísima Concepción de Acuña.

Begin your visit with a stop at the modern visitors center to pick up a free Park Service brochure (a necessity for driving the Mission Trail), then start your self-guided tour of the chapel. The flagstone floor has borne thousands of worshippers, from barefooted Indians two centuries ago to tennis-shoed tourists today. Indeed, be sure that you do wear tennis shoes, or some type of sturdy walking shoes, for the mission tours. All the sites have irregular staircases and stone walkways that are especially slippery on rainy days.

Mission Concepción is especially notable for its wall paintings. Geometric and religious symbols in ochre, blue, and brown decorate the ceilings and walls of several rooms. The most striking is the image once called the "Eye of God," through cleaning now revealed to be a face emanating rays of light. Displays at each of the four missions illustrate different aspects of mission life. At Concepción, the theme is "The Mission as a Religious Center," appropriate for a place known as one of the oldest unrestored stone churches as well as the oldest unrestored Catholic church in the nation.

Like the Alamo just over two miles to the north, Mission Concepción saw its own share of bloodshed. On October 28, 1835, Colonel James Bowie and 20 Texans were surprised by a detachment of the Mexican army. They fought well and forced the Mexicans, with 60 dead and 40 wounded, to retreat. The Texans only suffered one loss, further bolstering their spirits. Less than five months later, however, Bowie and his men would again fight the Mexican army, with far less success.

The second mission stop on the trail is the grandest in terms of size and architectural detail, so much so, in fact, that it was termed "Queen of the Missions." In its heyday **Mission San José** (6539 San Jose Dr., 210-229-4770) boasted 300 residents, a granary that held 5,000 bushels of corn, and elaborate ornamentation. Its full name is San José y San Miguel de Agüayo, named for the Governor of Coahuila and Texas at the time of its founding.

You may find yourself humming "Do You Know the Way to San Jose?" when traveling the mission route to this second site. The route mapped by the Park Service is the most scenic but not the most direct. Just follow the signs, and be patient; when you do reach San Jose, the drive will have been worth the effort. Thanks to an extensive renovation in 1936 for the Texas Centennial, this mission is in spectacular condition. The elegant structure echoes with reminders of an earlier time, when Texas was a frontier and this mission was a haven in an unsettled land. The most famous detail here is "Rosa's Window." Legend has it that a carpenter named Pedro Huizar created the window for his lost love, Rosa. (When you're downtown, look at the Dillard's exterior window displays at the Rivercenter Mall. These are copies of Rosa's Window, built for the former Joske's store.)

Walk around the grounds to get an idea of the size of this former community. Indians lived in rooms along the outside wall, and the priests lived in the two-story *convento*. The land in the quadrangle was used as a work area. The theme of San José is "The Mission as Social Center and a Center for Defense." A diorama located in the granary details a day in the life of those living at the mission.

Continue south along mission trail and you'll soon pass Espada Park and Acequia Parks. (Skip this route on rainy days.) Picnic tables afford a good place to take a scenic break halfway through the trail. The San Antonio River winds between these parks. At one time, *acequias* wound along both sides of the river; today only the one in Espada Park is active. **Mission San Juan** (9102 Graff Rd., 210-229-5734), fully named San Juan Capistrano, was once completely self-sustaining, supplying all its own needs from cloth to crops. San Juan provided not only for its own agricultural needs, but it also supplied other communities in the area. Skilled artisans made ironwork and leather goods and wove cloth in the workshops.

To appreciate the natural richness of this area, take a hike on the San Juan Woodlands Trail. In about one-third of a mile, the trail winds along the low river bottom land and gives you a look at some of the plants used by the inhabitants of the mission.

The chapel, with its bell tower and elaborate altar, was severely damaged by a storm in 1886. In 1909 the building was repaired and in the 1960s it underwent an extensive renovation. Today this is an active parish church and a good example of continuing community at San Antonio's historic mission structures.

San Juan also has a small **museum** featuring items found at the site and artifacts typically used by missionaries in Texas. The theme of San Juan is "The Mission as an Economic Center," and displays show how this self-sufficient mission worked with others to provide food and goods.

From Mission San José, head west on Mission Road to Ashley, turn left, then right on Espada Road. This will take you to the most remote spot on the trail: **Mission Espada** (10040 Espada, 210-627-2021). Located about nine miles from the downtown area, this mission was named for St. Francis of Assisi, founder of the order of Franciscans. The mission's full name is Mission San Francisco de la Espada.

This mission's theme is "The Mission as a Vocational Education Center," carried out through displays and demonstrations on the education of the Indians in blacksmithing, woodworking, and other vocational areas.

SHOPPING

San José is home to the only gift shop in the missions, with the exception of the Alamo. **Los Compadres Gift Shop** (210-922-0360) offers three rooms of Latin American crafts and collectibles. Look for folk art from Guatemala, Mexico, and Peru at this interesting shop. Tin art, Dia de los Muertos (Day of the Dead) figurines, Taxco silver jewelry, and religious medals are sold here.

This mission also has an excellent bookstore, the **Spanish Colonial Bookstore** (210-921-7220). History buffs can browse for hours through the collection of Texas and Mexican history. If you're looking for information about Spanish missions in Texas and all across the Southwest, this is the place to go.

DINING

At the start of Mission Trail, **Magnolia Station** (800 S. Alamo, 210-223-5353; $, □) serves a varied cuisine in a casual atmosphere. Have a burger or taco salad for lunch, or go all out with a dinner of Cajun fried catfish, New York strip steak, or shrimp shish kabob.

MARKET SQUARE

All of San Antonio enjoys a Tex-Mex atmosphere, a blend of cultures that come together in each aspect of everyday life. But nowhere in the city is this as evident as at Market Square. Here Texas and Mexico join hands to offer unique shopping, some of the city's finest Tex-Mex dining, joyful fiestas scheduled year-round, and an overall appeal that draws both visitors and residents alike.

Bounded by Interstate 35 and Santa Rosa, Dolorosa, and Commerce Streets, this two-block area embraces three special shopping centers: Farmer's Market, a recently renovated former produce market now ripe with crafts and imports after a $2.1 million renovation; an open-air consortium of specialty boutiques; and El Mercado, the largest Mexican market in the United States.

The history of Market Square dates back to the early 1800s, to a time when Mexico ruled the settlement of San Antonio de Bejar. Fresh produce and meats were sold in the Farmer's Market, and pharmaceutical items were available at Botica Guadalupana, today the oldest continuously operated pharmacy in town. However, the market's real claim to fame lies in the fact that it was the birthplace of *chili con carne,* the spicy meat and bean mixture that today is generally considered the state dish of Texas. Once young girls known as "chili queens" sold the concoction from small stands in the market.

El Mercado offers any kind of item that shoppers typically find in a Mexican border town. Styled after a traditional Mexican *mercado* or market, this one is enclosed and air conditioned, with merchandise piled to the ceiling. Look for onyx chess sets, ashtrays, painted pottery, silver jewelry, sombreros, and charro hats. The prices here are slightly higher than those found in Mexican border towns and, unlike the fare offered in traditional *mercados,* the merchandise carries set prices. Prices vary from store to store within the market, and most shops accept major credit cards.

Clothing and textiles are always best-sellers at El Mercado. The traditional Mexican dress, complete with an embroidered bodice and short sleeves, starts at about $35. When choosing a quality garment, look for tight embroidery stitches. Men's shirts, called *guayaberas,* are found throughout the stores as well. These solid-color, short-sleeved shirts, decorated with pleating and stitching, are worn outside the pants.

Blankets are another popular item. Many stores sell striped

ones in a variety of sizes and colors, most made from a wool blend. A five-by-seven-foot blanket typically costs $7 to $8; *panchos* and *serapes* sell for $10 to $12.

Piñatas are found throughout Market Square. At Mexican birthday parties, one of these colorful paper creations is filled with candy and hung from a tree. Blindfolded children take turns swinging at the vessel with a stick until someone finally breaks it and the loot spills all over the ground. Look for *piñatas* in the shapes of watermelons, clowns, donkeys, and even parrots.

Cascarones, dyed eggshells filled with paper confetti and covered with tissue paper, are sold in many stores. They're especially popular during the annual Fiesta, when children break them over the heads of their friends (or sometimes complete strangers).

DINING

Mi Tierra (218 Produce Row, 210-225-1262; $, □) is the restaurant that never sleeps. Twenty-four hours a day, 365 days a year, this San Antonio institution serves up some of the city's best Tex-Mex fare. No matter when you visit, Mi Tierra is packed with locals and visitors. They crowd into this festive eatery, into booths garnished year-round with Christmas decorations, to enjoy Mi Tierra's specialties.

Breakfast is a busy time, and locals start their day here with *huevos rancheros, chiliquiles* (scrambled eggs mixed with cheese, onions, and strips of corn tortillas, served with refried beans), or breakfast tacos. All feature the best tortillas in San Antonio. For lunch, Tex-Mex delights fill the menu: *enchiladas, carne asada, quesadillas.* Strolling troubadours take requests for Mexican ballads and give the restaurant a truly authentic air. Just as authentic is the adjacent *panaderia,* a Mexican bakery exuding its own tasty aromas: fresh tortillas and *polvorones,* cookies topped with cinnamon and sugar.

Just around the corner from Mi Tierra is its sister restaurant, **La Margarita** (120 Produce Row, 210-227-7140; $, □). This restaurant was established to accommodate the huge overflow of Mi Tierra customers, but today it draws a regular clientele of its own. Fajitas are the specialty at this often-noisy restaurant, and they're served with spicy *pico de gallo,* a mixture of chopped onions, cilantro, and peppers strong enough to wake up any palate. If you choose al fresco dining at this establishment, you can enjoy watching shoppers stroll among the many specialty shops and vendor carts.

ATTRACTIONS

The **Spanish Governor's Palace** (105 Plaza de Armas, 210-224-0601; small admission fee) is located just down the street from Market Square. Don't expect a palace in the usual sense of the word—turrets and towers are replaced by a simple patio and courtyard here. Remember, this dates back to the early 18th century, a time when the area was wild and unsettled, and this place was considered quite ornate, comparatively speaking. Built for officials of New Spain, today it's the only remaining example in Texas of an early aristocratic Spanish home.

Nearby, the **Jose Navarro Home** (228 S. Laredo St., 210-226-4801; admission fee) was the former residence of a signer of the Texas Declaration of Independence. The adobe and limestone structure includes an office used by Navarro, who was a lawyer and legislator. Today the historic home is open Wednesday through Saturday.

For many years, folks believed the **San Fernando Cathedral** (115 Main Plaza, 210-227-1297) was the final resting place of the defenders of the Alamo. A Spanish church was built at this site in 1738 by the city's Canary Island colonists. Here Santa Anna raised a flag of "no quarter" before he stormed the Alamo, signifying to the Texians (the pre-Revolution Texans) that he would take no prisoners. In 1873, following a fire after the Civil War, the chapel was replaced with the present-day construction. Although a tomb holds the remains of some unknown soldiers, modern historians do not believe these were the bodies of the Alamo defenders because evidence of military uniforms, never worn by the Texians, has turned up among the remains.

SHOPPING

Rivera's Chili Shop (109½ S. Concho, 210-226-9106) recalls Market Square's early chili connection with chili peppers, dried chiles, chili clothing, and even chili Christmas decorations. Look for Texas cookbooks and specialty foods here as well.

One of Market Square's most interesting shops is the **Dagen-Bela Ortiz Galeria** (102 Concho, 210-225-0731). Here you'll find upscale gift items from both the Southwest and Mexico. This two-story gallery features unique jewelry, folk art, and bronzes by Victor Gutierrez.

Locals and vacationers alike shop at **The Tequila Tree** (202 Produce Row, 210-224-6202). This three-story shop sells imports from around the world, from scarves made in Nepal to religious figures created in Guatemala. Nearly 40 countries are represented here through jewelry, clothing, and artwork.

ACCOMMODATIONS

Directly across from Market Square stands **La Quinta Market Square** (900 Dolorosa, 210-271-0001 or 800-531-5900; $$, ☐). This comfortable motel is built around an open-air patio with a pool and towering palms. The rooms are comfortable though not fancy—perfect for vacationing families.

Two blocks from Market Square, the **Holiday Inn Market Square** (318 W. Durango, 210-225-3211 or 800-HOLIDAY; $$–$$$, ☐) has 300-plus guest rooms as well as an Olympic-sized swimming pool and a full-service Mexican restaurant.

BROADWAY

Travel north from downtown on Broadway and you'll be journeying to some of San Antonio's top attractions. The stars you'll see on Broadway here include many of the most family-oriented sites in the city. The route weaves through downtown, past numerous car dealerships, before reaching Brackenridge Park. The largest park in the city, this one sprawls across 433 acres shaded by majestic live oaks.

Brackenridge Park is a fine place for a picnic or a stroll, but for many visitors it's also a major destination because of the many attractions found there. Families should budget at least half a day, for example, to visit the zoo. Garden lovers, too, will find a wealth of sites to explore. Brackenridge Park is home to the Japanese Tea Gardens, and nearby San Antonio Botanical Gardens and the Halsell Conservatory display plants from the Lone Star State and from around the globe.

If the weather is bad (or you're ready for a break from a hot summer day), take in a museum. Several off-Broadway choices offer exhibits ranging from the Texas Rangers to fine art.

ATTRACTIONS

Brackenridge Park (2800 N. Broadway, two miles north of downtown) is a definite stop for families. The **San Antonio Zoological Garden and Aquarium** (3903 N. St. Mary's St., 210-734-7183; admission fee) is widely considered one of the best zoos in the nation. Housed in a former rock quarry, the exhibits here are tucked back beside limestone cliffs and fed by artesian springs.

The zoo is best known for its excellent collection of African antelopes as well as other hoofed species. You'll find many other popular favorites, too, from African lions to Asian elephants and from snow leopards to giant armadillos. Over 2,500 animals representing 700 species are exhibited here. Birds, including many housed in open-air exhibits, make up a large part of the collection. San Antonio holds the distinction as the only zoo in the nation with a pair of whooping cranes who have successfully bred in captivity.

The **Children's Zoo,** a $3 million addition, features rides and exhibits to delight younger visitors. A nursery, desert building, playground, and education center comprise this new section. The highlight of the Children's Zoo is the "Round-the-World Voyage of Discovery." Step aboard a family-sized boat for a cruise that takes in tortoises, waterfowl, and even sharks!

Other children's attractions are sprinkled throughout Brackenridge Park. A **miniature railroad** (3810 N. St. Mary's St., 210-736-9534; small admission fee) runs 3½ miles through the park. Every train is a replica of an 1863 C. P. Huntington model. Kids also love the **carousel** (3910 N. St. Mary's St., 210-734-5401; small admission fee).

Your best view of the park comes aboard the **Skyride** (3910 N. St. Mary's St., 210-299-8480; small admission fee). Catch a ride on these bubble-shaped cars near the zoo entrance.

Yippee-ti-yi-ay! If you've always wanted to ride a horse down a Texas trail, here's your chance—even if that trail just winds through Brackenridge Park. The **Brackenridge Stables** (840 E. Mulberry Ave., 210-732-8881) offer individual rides for 20 to 45 minutes. Pony rides are available for younger buckaroos.

You'll see plenty of horse-related exhibits at the **Pioneer Memorial Hall** (3805 Broadway, 210-822-9011; admission fee). This museum traces the role of the Texas Rangers on the frontier, with exhibits covering badges to saddlebags. Western art is displayed here as well.

Just as the San Antonio Zoo utilizes the former rock quarry, so do the **Japanese Tea Gardens** (3800 N. St. Mary's, 210-299-3000; free). San Antonio's semitropical climate encourages the lush flowers, climbing vines, and tall palms found inside this quiet, serene place. The ponds, with beautiful rock bridges and walkways, are home to hundreds of koi (large goldfish).

This limestone quarry was transformed into a garden in 1918, when fish ponds and a palm-thatched arbor were featured in the development. Later, a pagoda was added and a Japanese-American couple operated a tea room nearby. In World War II, public pressure forced the family to move, and the tea room was taken over by a Chinese family. The attraction was renamed the Chinese Tea Gardens. Recently, descendants of the former Japanese-American proprietors, along with the Japanese ambassador to the United States, were hosted as the gardens were officially renamed the Japanese Tea Gardens.

Garden lovers should save time for the **San Antonio Botanical Gardens and Halsell Conservatory** (555 Funston Place, 210-821-5115; admission fee). Roses, herbs, a garden for the blind, and native plants are found within the lovely setting of these 38-acre gardens, the centerpiece of which is the Halsell Conservatory.

HIDDEN TREASURES:
THE LUCILE HALSELL CONSERVATORY

No one would deny that Texas summers are painfully, sometimes almost unbearably hot—even for Texas natives. For visitors from cooler climates, however, the 100-plus degree temperatures can mean death—especially when that "visitor" is a delicate edelweiss from the Swiss Alps or a fragile fern from the Pacific Northwest.

In the past, gardeners of Central and South Texas have known that the greenhouses and conservatories that were a blessing to their northern neighbors could do more harm than good in this semitropical climate. Greenhouses meant a long battle to keep plants alive through hours of hot summer sunshine and high temperatures that were only escalated by panes of glass. But the San Antonio Botanical Society came up with a Texas-sized solution to the odd dilemma of how to build a conservatory that would minimize, rather than maximize, sunlight and heat. The answer: the Lucile Halsell Conservatory, a $6.9 million project.

This 90,000-square-foot conservatory is an architectural masterpiece designed by Emilio Ambasz, formerly Curator of Design at New York's Museum of Modern Art. Ambasz created a new definition for the conservatory, choosing a form that's as functional as it is eye-catching. The Halsell Conservatory departs from the house-shape of typical conservatories, relying instead on conical and triangular roof shapes that rise from the buildings like jagged steel and glass splinters. The seven tall glass spires that surround a center courtyard soar to the height of a five-story building, giving the conservatory a futuristic look. And there's one other interesting detail—the entire project is built underground.

To take advantage of the cooling effect of the earth, the greenhouse is built 16 feet underground. Unlike a typical conservatory, where glazing serves as the walls and the roof, the Halsell Conservatory contains glazing only on the angled roofs. The conservatory blends in so well with the rolling hills that surround the structure that many visitors never realize they are underground. The descent is slow and gradual, spread out through two entrance rooms.

The entrance to the conservatory is a ramp that feeds into

the first exhibit area—a concrete passageway containing the Alpine Room. This tiny exhibit behind a glass viewing wall, the only nonaccessible exhibit in the conservatory, contains delicate Alpine fauna such as the famous edelweiss and the Alpine sunflower. This may look like an ordinary exhibit, but it's definitely high tech. Refrigeration tubes in the soil and in the air can drop the temperature to freezing. Lighting in the Alpine room is artificial to simulate daylight intensities at various latitudes where the plants originate.

But the Alpine Room is just a taste of the uniqueness that makes this conservatory special. Continue the gradual descent into the conservatory through the breathtaking Exhibit Hall. This circular garden, with its ever-changing display of color, features flowers with a seasonal tie-in, including Easter lilies, Christmas poinsettias, and fall mums. To facilitate display changes, the plants are kept in their pots, buried in a bed of sand. Gardeners can quickly pull the pots and replace wilting specimens with new ones chosen from over 25,000 square feet of plants kept in a growing area near the conservatory.

The Exhibit Hall is one of the glass structures that provides controlled light to delicate plants. Here, as in the other conservatory rooms, temperature and humidity are read mechanically and automatically fed into a central computer that controls the very different environments of the separate areas. Specially constructed "shades" are found in each area that, when told by the computer to limit light, automatically stretch over the glazed areas to diminish the sunshine entering the room. The glass roofs of the separate conservatory rooms each present a unique shape—from cones to triangles. Although architecturally pleasing, the roof lines were designed with a far more practical consideration in mind: minimizing the harmful effects of sun and wind.

The Desert Room sustains one of the most extreme environments found here. Visitors feel the blast of warm air as they enter the glass doors of the pavilion. Like tall sentinels throwing their arms up in surrender, the giant saguaros stand watch over their bizarre neighbors. The cacti come in many different shapes from skinny pencil varieties to the round barrel types, and their names are quite colorful—chocolate drop, strawberry, and rainbow. Don't miss the Queen Agave Cactus from Mexico.

Continued

It's hard to overlook, with each spine measuring over four inches long.

Be ready for a complete change of climate in the gardens of the Gretchen Northrup Tropical Conservatory, a complete jungle paradise save for the slither of a snake or the raucous call of an exotic bird. The room brims with greenery, ranging from the scarlet plume from Mexico to Bolivia's red powderpuff. Plants from as far away as India and Cambodia also flourish in this humid tropical space. The exotic blossoms here provide a special treat, filling the room with their own heady fragrance and bursts of color among the greenery. Look for orchids, hibiscus, and bromeliads scattered throughout the display, and pause for a moment at the small waterfall and reflection pool in the center of the room.

After a visit to the dense tropical room it's almost a shock to step into the airy Palm House—a five-story conical structure that dominates the conservatory. The wide, 110-foot base is planted with palms and cycads from the New World, including Florida's royal palm, the saw palmetto from the Southeastern United States, and the South American queen palm. At the top of the Palm House, step outside for a bird's-eye view of the conservatory. From this vantage point, it's easy to see what's hidden at the front entrance: the fact that the conservatory is truly an underground building. Off in the distance you can view the skyscrapers of downtown San Antonio.

Perhaps the most popular room of the conservatory is the greenery-filled Fern Room. The focal point here is the double-tier waterfall and large pond planted with lilies. Enjoy a cool (but damp!) walk behind the waterfall as you circle the crowded room. Exotic plants such as bear's foot fern from Malaysia, climbing fern from China, and tailflower from tropical America grow alongside giant elephant ears and Hawaiian fern trees in the lushest of the conservatory's environments.

Military buffs should stop by the adjacent **Fort Sam Houston** (N. New Braunfels Ave. and Stanley Rd., 210-221-6117; free) for a self-guided tour. This National Historic Landmark, an army base dating back to 1870, has nine times as many historic buildings as Colonial Williamsburg. These include the residence where General John J. Pershing lived in 1917; the Chinese Camp, once occupied by Chinese who fled Mexico to escape Pancho Villa; and the home where Lieutenant and Mrs. Dwight Eisenhower lived in 1916. Visitors can stroll past the structures (which are not open to the public). The post also includes two museums. The **Fort Sam Houston Museum** (210-221-1886; free) is filled with exhibits on the site's early days. It is open Wednesday through Sunday. The **U.S. Army Medical Department Museum** (210-221-6358; free) houses exhibits on military medical practices dating back to the Revolutionary War. This museum is open Wednesday through Saturday.

Families with small children will want to visit **Kiddie Park** (3015 Broadway, 210-824-4351). Since 1925 kids have squealed on the Ferris wheel and the "Little Dipper" roller coaster and relaxed on the antique merry-go-round. Rides are inexpensive here, just 25 to 45 cents a whirl, and the operators call this the oldest kiddie park in the nation.

Another attraction in this area is an off-Broadway show—on North New Braunfels Avenue, to be exact. The **Marion Koogler McNay Museum** (6000 N. New Braunfels Ave., 210-824-5368; free) is a joy to behold, not just because of its collection but also because of the building that contains it. This was the home of Marion Koogler McNay, heiress to an oil fortune and an artist herself. Built in the 1920s, the 24-room house was converted to a museum in the 1950s. Today it houses an extensive collection that McNay acquired over the years. The world's finest artists, from Gauguin to Picasso to Manet, grace the walls of this museum's numerous galleries. The McNay is open Tuesday through Sunday (Sunday afternoon only), but closed on Monday.

Another premier art collection also beckons off Broadway—the **San Antonio Museum of Art** (200 W. Jones Ave., 210-978-8100; admission fee), which is housed in the former Lone Star Brewery. A $7.2 million grant transformed this former factory into a museum for the permanent display of artwork ranging from Greek antiquities and pre-Columbian sculpture to 18th-, 19th-, and 20th-century paintings.

For a look at the natural history of Texas, plan a visit to the **Witte Museum** (3801 Broadway, 210-820-2111; admission fee). This exciting museum, a favorite with children for its interactive exhibits, covers all things Texan, from the area's dinosaur inhabitants to the white-tailed deer that roam the region today.

SHOPPING

If you want to look like a real cowboy, you'll need a Western hat. Since 1917, **Paris Hatters** (119 Broadway, 210-223-3453) has outfitted cowboys and cowboy wanna-bes with Stetson and Resistol hats.

Of course, every cowboy also needs boots, and you can get those at **Lucchese Boot Company** (4025 Broadway, 210-828-9419). For over a century, this company has been making Western boots, including many from exotic leathers such as alligator and ostrich.

DINING

Looking for barbecue? You've come to the right part of town. Two of the finest barbecue joints await hungry visitors on Broadway.

The **Club House Pit Bar-B-Q** (2218 Broadway, 210-229-9945; $, □) is one of the real treasures of San Antonio. This family owned and operated joint serves up slow-cooked barbecue prepared in a brick pit. All the meats are prepared without tenderizers or MSG—what you see is what you get, with lots of tangy sauce. You can choose from ribs (both pork and beef), all-beef sausage, chicken, pork, and beef brisket. Can't decide? Choose the "Super Platter" with a combination of five meats, potato salad, beans, and white bread. It's the best buy in the house and truly Texas-sized. Finally, if anyone has saved room, there's a good supply of desserts. Offerings vary, but you'll usually find peach cobbler, brownies, bread pudding, and even sweet potato pie.

Paul Bunyan appetites should come by on Tuesday or Friday evenings for the all-you-can-eat special. On Friday nights, besides the all-you-can-eat offering, there's live jazz, too, usually with no cover charge.

Down the street, **Billy Blues Bar and Grill** (330 E. Grayson, 210-225-7409; $–$$, □) is a San Antonio–based chain of roadhouse barbecue joints with locations in Austin, Dallas, and Houston. Billy's menu is big, starting with "Warm Up Acts" that include "Wings and a Prayer" (barbecued chicken wings), "Lightnin' Bolts" (battered jalapeño peppers), and "Gimme Caps" (fried mushrooms). From there, choose a "Pinched Piggy Sandwich" for tender pulled pork shoulder, a "Hard Luck Club" for a barbecue club sandwich, or your usual beef brisket, smoked sausage, or chopped beef sandwich.

This popular eatery hosts musicians from San Antonio and Austin plus nationally known acts. Blues rules, but two nights a week are reserved for jazz and acoustic acts.

You'll also find barbecue, plus sandwiches, salads, and soups, at the **Pig Stand** (1508 Broadway, 210-222-2794; $). The Pig Stand calls itself the "world's first drive-in." Its first location was in Dallas, built in 1921, and the San Antonio site was constructed shortly after on Broadway. When the highway interchange project took place a few years ago, the original building was condemned and the restaurant was moved a few hundred yards away, but they're still serving the pig sandwiches, burgers, and malts that made them famous.

Another long-standing San Antonio tradition awaits right down the road. **Earl Abel's** (4200 Broadway, 210-822-3358; $, □) has been serving folks for over half a century in a no-frills diner. Like a comfortable pair of sneakers, there's something soothing about Earl Abel's and its dependable menu that starts with a good old-fashioned scrambled egg and pancake breakfast and continues with Texas favorites such as burgers, chicken-fried steak, and fried chicken.

AIRPORT

Even though your visit to San Antonio may be brief and you're staying near the airport, take heart. Unlike some cities, where the airport is miles from the center of town, San Antonio International is situated on the north side of town off Loop 410, an upscale area just a quick drive from good shopping and dining.

Loop 410 circles the entire city, but this stretch has the lion's share of the loop's retail businesses. Some serious shoppers arrive in San Antonio and never venture beyond the loop, spending their stay in mega North Star Mall or the nearby Central Park Mall. Many shoppers from Mexico make annual trips to San Antonio just to browse through these malls.

SHOPPING

Just below the traffic lies **Los Patios** (2015 N.E. Loop 410, 210-655-6171), a quiet retreat in the heart of the hustle and bustle of the Loop. This 20-acre open-air mall is filled with specialty shops, from **Tejas Gifts** for Texas souvenirs to **Tienda** for Mexican jewelry and south of the border items. The shopping area also has three indoor/outdoor restaurants. But, as excellent as its shopping is, the real charm of Los Patios lies in its setting. Located on the banks of Salado Creek, the retail area is nestled within majestic live oaks and exotic plants.

Shopping is more cosmopolitan at **North Star Mall** (210-340-6627), the priciest mall in town. With anchor stores that include Saks Fifth Avenue, Marshall Field's, and Foley's, you'll find the best money can buy here. North Star Mall is easy to spot on the Loop—just look for the boots. This 40-foot tall pair of cowboy footwear was the creation of sculptor Robert Wade.

DINING

Take a break from your shopping with lunch at the **Gazebo** (Los Patios Shopping Center, 210-655-6190; $, ☐). Featuring both indoor and outdoor seating, this restaurant serves up salads and sandwiches to satiate shoppers.

For Tex-Mex treats, head to the **Alamo Cafe** (9714 San Pedro, 210-341-4526; $, ☐.) This favorite with locals specializes in enchilada dinners, including beef, chicken, cheese, and sour cream, as well as fajitas, chicken-fried steaks, and other Texas favorites.

ACCOMMODATIONS

The airport area is dotted with accommodations, including family-priced properties such as **La Quinta Airport West** (219 N.E. Loop 410, 210-342-4291 or 800-531-5900; $, □), the **Drury Inn Airport** (143 N.E. Loop 410, 210-366-4300 or 800-325-8300; $, □), and the **Ramada Inn Airport** (1111 N.E. Loop 410, 210-828-9031 or 800-228-2828; $, □). Other hotels have targeted the more luxury-conscious traveler, such as the **Sheraton Fiesta** (37 N.E. Loop 410, 210-366-2424 or 800-325-3535; $$$, □) and the **San Antonio Airport Hilton** (611 N.W. Loop 410, 210-340-6060 or 800-445-8667; $$, □).

FAR NORTHWEST

Northwest of the city limits, San Antonio quickly gives way to the Hill Country. Houses become fewer. City blocks trail off, replaced by barbed wire fences. The countryside, now rolling with rocky hills, is dotted with live oak trees. This is the Texas Hill Country, and it lies just beyond Loop 1604, the outside circle around San Antonio. The Loop begins near I-35 as a major highway, dwindling on the west side of the city to little more than a farm-to-market road.

This area is home to San Antonio's most family-oriented attractions: Pear Apple County Fair, Fiesta Texas, and Sea World of Texas. Pear Apple Country is a pay-per-ride amusement park that's popular with both local children and visitors. The two theme parks draw guests from around the country as well as Mexico to test their courage on daredevil roller coasters, cool off in water parks, enjoy world-class shows, and learn more about marine life. Each also has special areas for small children under 42 inches tall.

Fiesta Texas operates in a former limestone quarry. The white, chalky stone used to build homes throughout Central and South Texas was mined from this and similar sites, leaving behind tall limestone cliffs that make dramatic backdrops for the park. San Antonio has a long history of reusing its quarries: the San Antonio Zoo and the Japanese Tea Gardens occupy a former quarry, using the walls to contain animals and grow subtropical vines.

Rather than being competitive, San Antonio's two theme parks are actually complementary. Fiesta Texas showcases music, from '50s rock 'n roll and local *Tejano* sounds to oompah German tunes. Award-winning shows are interspersed with thrill rides, sure to bring a squeal to even the most jaded amusement park goers.

Sea World of Texas, the largest in the Sea World chain, is a marine park that offers equal emphasis on education and fun. Displays and shows featuring orcas, dolphins, seals, and otters partner with an enjoyable water park.

Allow at least a one-day visit for each park. During the heat of the Texas summer, when temperatures topping 100 degrees are not unusual, consider arriving early, returning to your motel in the afternoon for a swim and a chance to rest, and then venturing back in the evening. If you want to remain in the park all day, plan to move slowly, drink plenty of fluids, and rest often. Heat exhaustion is a real danger in this part of the country, so pace yourself.

PEAR APPLE COUNTY FAIR

Local families and vacationing ones as well who are looking for an afternoon outing head to **Pear Apple County Fair** (5820 N.W. Loop 410 between Ingram and Bandera Rds., 210-521-9500; free admission, charge for rides). Spanning 15 acres, this amusement park offers both indoor and outdoor games and rides. Kids can take a turn on the indoor Ferris wheel, ride the train, or bounce around on bumper cars. There's a ⅔-mile go-cart track and two 18-hole miniature golf courses to keep others busy and happy. Cost varies by rides, but getting into the park is free.

FIESTA TEXAS

What makes Texas special? Its many cultures and its rich history. Fiesta Texas takes both elements, combines them with a sprinkle of song and a dash of daredevil rides, and comes up with a top-notch theme park. This park features sections that highlight Texas's rich diversity, from Mexican and German sections to a part that celebrates the Lone Star State's rip-roarin' Western past.

Fiesta Texas is located at the intersection of I-10 West and Loop 1604. You'll enter the park through **Los Festivales,** styled with stucco buildings and rich with the atmosphere of Texas's closest neighbor. Wandering musicians play festive mariachi music and open-air shows feature *Tejano* and *conjunto* music. You won't find rides in this section, but you will see the park's largest theater: Teatro Zaragoza. A great place to save for the heat of the afternoon, the theater is home to the Festival Folklorico show, with swirling Mexican dances and traditional songs.

Los Festivales also provides a taste of Old Mexico. Pick up some *churros* (deep-fried dough doused with sugar) and roasted corn, or, if you're ready to take a break, enjoy a meal in the Mi Pueblito restaurant (reservations are accepted).

If you are a roller coaster fan, then you know about **Crackaxle Canyon.** This Western section is the home of "The Rattler," the world's tallest wooden roller coaster. Lines can be long for this popular ride, so head here early for a jump on the crowds.

How can we write about The Rattler? Only by having boarded the 2½-minute dynamo.

The Rattler is not for everybody. John quickly decided that he fell into that category. Paris boarded the coaster, and then spent the remainder of that Fiesta Texas visit trying to get the ground to stop moving. (On a positive note, we found that Fiesta Texas personnel are wonderfully helpful—even to guests a little green around the gills.) So, to give readers a better picture of The Rattler, we sent our young apprentices: Liz, 16, and Lauren, 13. Here is Lauren's evaluation, so decide for yourself if this ride's for you:

My sister warned me to close my eyes as we were about to plunge down the tallest wooden roller coaster in the world, the Rattler. Bravely, I kept my eyes open and held on as we began the drop. I remembered how my sister had talked me into going on the Rattler, and I realized how much I would have missed if I hadn't.

The Rattler is definitely a great roller coaster. Fiesta Texas takes everyone's picture while they are on the Rattler. I saw ours. My eyes were bulging out of my head, and my mouth was curved in a smile. My sister's head was down, and she couldn't get it back up because of the speed of this exciting roller coaster.

If you decide that you're not Rattler material, there are plenty of other reasons to stop in Crackaxle Canyon. Sit in the shade and listen to the sounds of today's top country-western songs sung by talent collected from around the country. Or take a wet ride on the "Gully Washer" or jump aboard the train for an overview of the park. Also in Crackaxle Canyon, you can have a taste of real Texas barbecue at Old Blue's Original Style BBQ.

The **water park** is a top draw on hot summer afternoons. You'll need a swimsuit for most rides (shorts are not permitted), and lockers are available for wet items. Here you'll find the theme park's coolest rides, splashing thrillers with names like "The Twister," "The Six Chuter," and "The Gusher."

Fiesta Texas's newest section, inaugurated in 1994, is the **Boardwalk.** It's easy to find—just look for the Ferris wheel. A Texas version of Atlantic City's Boardwalk, this section features games of chance, a roller rink, a sand "beach" and a lake with games and paddleboats, and a fun carnival atmosphere. Unless you have a fear of heights, take a turn on the Ferris wheel, preferably at night. When the park is lit like a Christmas tree, you'll have an unbeatable view, including of the twinkling San Antonio skyline in the distance.

Much of the Texas Hill Country was settled by German immigrants, and their contribution is remembered at **Spassburg.** The center of this section is a large beer hall where oompah bands play and perform the chicken dance several times daily. The hall is open all day, and families will welcome its fast food court and air-conditioned dining room. Next to the beer hall, you can board the train for a round-trip look at the entire park or a ride to Crackaxle Canyon on the far side. Spassburg is also home to the children's section, with an airplane ride, kiddie bumper cars, and a carousel.

Return to the days of bobby socks and poodle skirts at **Rockville,** the '50s section. Buddy Holly and Elvis Presley plus malt shops and drive-ins still live on in this fun section. Rockville is home to Fiesta Texas's most popular show: "Rockin' at Rockville High." This show fills up quickly, so pick up free tickets for the time of your choice as soon as you enter the park. If you need to cool down, head to the "Power Surge" in this section. Stand on the bridge to get completely drenched when the water coaster comes off the incline, or get in line (usually short) to experience this fun ride for yourself.

FOR MORE INFORMATION

Fiesta Texas is open seasonally March through November, with a limited schedule except during summer months. For more information, call (800) 473-4378.

SEA WORLD OF TEXAS

Sea World of Texas is located at the intersection of Elllison Drive and Westover Hills Boulevard, just off TX 151 between Loop 410 and Loop 1604.

Since its opening in April 1988, Sea World has packed in visitors eager to pet a porpoise, ogle an orca, or see a shark up close and personal. Sprawled across 250 acres northwest of the city, this Texas-sized park offers everything from marine shows to trick water-skiing performances, all amid acres of manicured gardens.

Make your first priority picking up a show schedule at the entrance pavilion. Sea World entertainment ranges from "The Pirates of the Pinniped" (showcasing the antics of sea lions and a Pacific walrus) to a show featuring Beluga whales and white-sided dolphins. Parrots and birds of prey have their own show, as does the park's human talent (at Water Ski Stadium).

The star of Sea World is **Shamu,** the 2½-ton orca who performs incredible leaps into the air and engages in graceful swimming exercises with his human partners. There's room for 4,500 onlookers in this stadium, and most of the seats are safe from the huge splashes that Shamu produces as he leaps and dives in his 7-million-gallon tank. Shamu performs with Grandbaby Shamu, born at the park in February 1993. A giant canvas roof shades spectators during hot South Texas days.

One of the most popular areas at Sea World is the **Penguin Exhibit,** featuring over 200 of the aquatic birds in a recreated Antarctic environment. Step aboard the moving sidewalk that glides by the penguins' glass enclosure for a close-up look at the icy rocks and cold water world that is home to these flightless fowl. The penguins glide around on their stomachs, dive from the rocks, waddle across the ice, and sometimes just stand and stare back at their visitors. If you can tear yourself away from these tuxedoed comedians, visit the next room for a look at videos on the different species and their behavior.

You'll find many exhibits at Sea World of Texas not seen at the other parks in the chain. The **coral reef display,** a giant 300,000-gallon exhibit, contains the world's largest collection of Indo-Pacific coral reef fishes in a simulated coral reef environment. Look for the lemon butterfly, the long-horned conefish, the yellow tang, and the spotted puffer, all swimming amongst the coral. The reef is realistic right down to the wave motion; from outside the exhibit you can see the wave maker at work.

Just past the coral reef you'll encounter the **shark tank,** where the park's most ferocious-looking residents dart from end to end in their large enclosure. The scalloped hammerhead, the blacktip, the nurse shark, and the lemon shark all eye their visitors from the confines of this 450,000-gallon habitat.

Although you'd probably rather not get much closer to the sharks, you will have a chance to reach out and touch some friendlier creatures at the **Marine Mammal Pool.** Pet an Atlantic bottlenose dolphin and, if you're around at afternoon feeding time, hand-feed one of these marine friends. Seals and sea lions along with North American river otters can also be fed and observed nearby.

San Antonio may be a long way from St. Louis, but as an Anheuser-Busch park, Sea World is home to some of the company's famous mascots: Clydesdale horses, each weighing over 2,300 pounds. An eight-horse team pulls a historic red wagon through the park several times each day.

Sea World of Texas boasts two gardens that provide quiet, thoughtful walkways among Texas flora and fauna. **Cypress Gardens West,** a 12-acre park planted with a continually changing display of flowers, is a miniature recreation of Cypress Gardens, the Florida member of the Sea World family. As you stroll along the paths, look for *doncellas,* Spanish maidens in traditional dress seated throughout the gardens.

Adjoining Cypress Gardens West, the **Texas Walk** offers visitors a chance to recall some of Texas's most prominent historical and contemporary citizens. Specially commissioned bronze statues are located throughout the walk, portraying dignitaries such as politicians Barbara Jordan and Henry B. Gonzales and author Katherine Anne Porter.

Children love Sea World, and they've been given their own area of the park located adjacent to the gardens. **Shamu's Happy Harbor** delights little ones with its nautically themed playscapes. Musical shows feature costumed versions of Shamu and friends.

Watching all this park's water activity may make you want to dive right in. Go ahead over at **Lost Lagoon,** a five-acre water park with everything from water slides to the "Sky Tubin'" water ride. Thrill seekers can take a five-story plunge on the "Texas Splashdown" or cool off under a soaking waterfall on the "Rio Loco," a "crazy river" that takes six people on circular rafts through white-water rapids.

FOR MORE INFORMATION

Sea World of Texas is open seasonally from March through October, with a limited schedule except during summer months. For more information, call (210) 523-3611.

ACCOMMODATIONS

Near the parks, the **Hyatt Hill Country Resort** (9800 Hyatt Resort Dr., 210-647-1234 or 800-233-1234; $$$, □) offers the area's most luxurious getaway. This 500-room resort nestles on 200 acres of a former cattle ranch, rolling land sprinkled with prickly pear cacti and live oaks. With its limestone architecture and Western decor, the four-story hotel has captured the atmosphere of the Hill Country, but it also incorporates the gingerbread trim featuring the Lone Star that often decorated homes of the German pioneers who settled this area.

The visual appeal starts with windmills and porch rockers outside and continues into the lobby with its massive stone fireplaces and Texas-style furniture. Guest rooms feature country elegance, from quilt-patterned bedspreads to windows that swing out for a cool fresh-air breeze. This resort is best known, though, for its outdoor amenities: an 18-hole championship golf course, tennis courts, and a four-acre water park. Cool off in one of two pools (family and adults only) separated by a waterfall, or grab an inner tube and float down the Ramblin' River, a man-made waterway that mimics a float down a Hill Country river.

TEXAS HILL COUNTRY

If you have a little extra time, spend a day or two in the Hill Country, a favorite getaway for San Antonio residents and a special part of Texas not to be missed.

Texas's richest vacation region was formed in less time than it takes to describe it. The Hill Country, a scenic area north and west of San Antonio, was shaped 30 million years ago by a violent 3½-minute earthquake. The convulsion buckled the earth and kicked up strata of limestone and granite into rugged hills and steep cliffs. The jagged scar of the event, the Balcones Escarpment, zigzags down the state, marking the frontier between flat farmland toward the east and rugged ranches to the west. Cotton and cornfields give way to hillsides dotted with limestone scrabble, textured by juniper and majestic live oaks, and tinted year-round by wildflowers.

The Hill Country is the true heart of Texas, and it offers one of the state's most popular vacation getaways. Ranches, wineries, state parks, resorts, and antique shops tempt travelers to escape from the Alamo City for a couple of days of country fun. The region is enormous, even by Texas standards. It spans 25,000 square miles and encompasses 23 counties. Fortunately, many Hill Country attractions are located within one or two hours of San Antonio, so even if you only have an afternoon free, you can venture out and enjoy some of the area's delights.

To head out into the Hill Country is to travel to small-town Texas, to a land where little has changed for generations. Many of these small communities were founded by immigrants who brought to their new country the language, traditions, and food of their homelands.

CASTROVILLE

One of these small towns is Castroville (210-538-3142), located 20 miles west of San Antonio on US 90. The distance may be short, but this is another world in terms of mood and atmosphere. Castroville presents a mixture of many cultures: French, German, English, Alsatian, and Spanish. Best known for its Alsatian roots, the town is sometimes called "The Little Alsace of Texas." The community was founded by Frenchman Henri Castro, who contracted with the Republic of Texas to bring settlers from Europe. These pioneers came from the French province of Alsace in 1844, bringing with them the Alsatian language, a Germanic dialect. Today only the older residents of Castroville carry on this mother tongue.

Although the language has dropped out of everyday use, many other Alsatian customs and traditions have survived. The city still sports European-style homes with nonsymmetrical, sloping roofs. The Alsatian Dancers of Texas perform folk dancing at many festivals, including San Antonio's Texas Folklife Festival in August (see "Festivals" at the back of this book). Castroville is a popular getaway for antiques shoppers, architecture and history buffs, and diners looking for a good German meal.

NEW BRAUNFELS

Another nearby town that has not forgotten its immigrant roots is New Braunfels (800-572-2626). Located 30 minutes northeast of San Antonio on I-35, New Braunfels retains its ties to the old country. Even today, don't be surprised to hear German spoken; it's still the main language in many local homes. Every October the town pulls out its *lederhosen* for one of the largest German festivals in the country. Wurstfest, a celebration of sausage making, is an event filled with oompah bands, bratwurst, and brew.

The Wurstfest grounds are located on the banks of the Comal River, which holds the title as the world's shortest river. It may be small, but the Comal packs a lot into its two miles. The headwaters are the Comal Springs, one of the largest springs in the state.

The spring waters of the Comal are cool, but the neighboring Guadalupe River is downright chilly. With a water temperature in the mid-50s, tubers still make the Guadalupe one of San Antonio's most popular day trips. On the "River Road" outside New Braunfels, river outfitters set up vacationers with inner tubes and transportation. From one of the drop-off points on the Guadalupe, you can drift beneath the tall cypress trees for hours.

Another way to enjoy the Guadalupe is at New Braunfels's **Schlitterbahn** (305 W. Austin St., 210-625-2351; admission fee), Texas's largest water park. With a German theme, the park offers stomach-churning thrill rides with names like "Der Bahn." For those seeking a slower pace, there's a huge hot tub and paddleboats on the river.

New Braunfels is known as the **"antiques capital of Texas,"** and it's easy to see why. Antique malls bulge with dozens of vendors, plus small one-room stores and warehouses of antiques are scattered all over town. Start your shopping tour at the New Braunfels Convention and Visitors Bureau (390 S. Seguin Ave, 800-445-2323) to pick up a brochure listing the numerous shops. Old World antiques and Texas primitives are sold throughout the town.

The German flavor of New Braunfels convinced the Nauer family of Switzerland that the city would be the perfect spot for the world's only museum featuring the art of Sister Maria Innocentia Hummel. Since World War II, the Nauer family has owned the works of this nun whose paintings inspired the popular Hummel figurines. Today the downtown **Hummel Museum** (199 Main Plaza, 800-456-4866; admission fee) displays artwork, figurines, Sister Hummel's personal belongings, and an extensive Hummel gift shop.

GRUENE

Shoppers should save time for a visit to Gruene (210-629-5077), once an independent community on the banks of the Guadalupe, now incorporated as part of New Braunfels. Rescued from its former status as a ghost town, Gruene is now filled with historic buildings that operate as antique shops, river outfitters, and even a winery. Pick up a free copy of "A Pedestrian Guide for Gruene Guests" at local shops, then head out to explore the historic buildings.

SAN MARCOS

Many shoppers make a special trip to San Marcos (800-782-7653 ext. 177), located half an hour beyond New Braunfels on north I-35. The reason? Well, there are over 100 reasons, all found right along the interstate. This is home to the **San Marcos Factory Shops** (800-628-9465), an open-air mall housing over 100 shops that sell direct from the factory. Luggage, shoes, leather goods, outdoor gear, china, kitchen goods, and other specialties are offered for sale. Nearby, the open-air **Tanger Factory Outlet Center** (512-396-7444) has over 30 shops featuring name brand designers and manufacturers. Shoppers can browse through housewares, footwear, home furnishings, leather goods, perfumes, and books.

Not all San Marcos attractions are man-made; the town is also known for its pure spring waters. The San Marcos River, which has been used by man for over 13,000 years, flows through town, providing the city with beautiful swimming and snorkeling spots. The river also serves as the home of **Aquarena Springs** (800-999-9767 or 512-396-8900), an amusement park with glass-bottomed boats, six rides, and shows built on the theme of the river and its history. The park's mascot, Ralph the Swimming Pig, performs daily at the submarine theater (the only one in the world, according to the park's owners). Nearby, you can have a look beneath the Hill Country at **Wonder Cave** (800-782-7653, ext. CAVE), a cavern created during a 3½-minute earthquake 30 million years ago. The same earthquake produced the Balcones Fault, an 1,800-mile line separating the western Hill Country from the flat eastern farmland.

FREDERICKSBURG

Shoppers and German aficionados will find buys, brews, and Bavarian meals in Fredericksburg (210-997-6523), northwest of San Antonio on US 290. Many of the town's accommodations are in historic Sunday houses, small two-story homes that distant farmers often owned in town so that they could spend Saturday afternoon at market, Saturday night in town, and Sunday morning at church.

Visitors can soak up history here not only in the bed-and-breakfasts and quaint shops, but also in a world-class museum, the **Admiral Nimitz State Historical Park** (340 E. Main St., 210-997-4379; admission fee). This historic park recalls the career of Admiral Chester Nimitz, World War II Commander-in-Chief of the Pacific (CinCPac) and Fredericksburg's most famous resident. Nimitz commanded 2.5 million troops from the time he assumed command 18 days after the attack on Pearl Harbor until the Japanese surrendered. Today this museum takes visitors back to the early days of Fredericksburg, when the building was the Steamboat Hotel owned by the Admiral's grandfather, and also back to World War II (several exhibits illustrate the Pacific campaign). Behind the museum lies the Garden of Peace, a classic Japanese garden that was a gift from the people of Japan.

JOHNSON CITY

History buffs should also make a trip to Johnson City (210-868-7684), the home of former president Lyndon Baines Johnson. Here you can have a look at two national historic parks plus the LBJ Ranch in nearby Stonewall.

In Johnson City, you can tour the **LBJ Boyhood Home.** LBJ was five years old in 1913 when his family moved to the simple frame house that still stands here. A nearby visitors center provides information on this site as well as on nearby Johnson Settlement and other LBJ attractions. You may also want to visit Stonewall, location of the **Texas White House.** Here bus tours take vacationers on tours of the ranch Johnson and Lady Bird called home. All the Johnson sites are free of charge, a stipulation of the late president.

KERRVILLE

Vacationers who come to Texas looking for the Wild West rather than an Old World atmosphere can find it in Kerrville (800-221-7958 in Texas or 210-792-3535). Located northwest of San Antonio on TX 16, Kerrville is home of the world famous **Y. O. Ranch,** which in the late 1800s grew to over 600,000 acres, covering a distance of 80 miles. The ranch was founded by Charles Schreiner, who became a Texas Ranger at the tender age of 15, and today his heirs still own the ranch, located outside of town in the community of Mountain Home.

Today the Y. O. Ranch remains a working ranch, raising Texas longhorn cattle, but it is also an exotic game ranch available for both hunting and photographic safaris. Guests can stay in century-old cabins or lodge rooms (210-640-3222; $$, □) or just visit for the day to enjoy a guided tour of the ranch (admission fee) and a look at the 50 exotic species who live there.

BANDERA

Follow TX 16 northwest for 50 miles to Bandera (800-364-3833), "The Cowboy Capital of the World." This town is well known for its plentiful ranches, country-western music, rodeos, and horse racing. Attention city slickers: Bandera's dude ranches will have you riding high in the saddle no matter what your equestrian experience.

Pleasures in the Hill Country are simple ones, the same kinds of diversions shared by pioneers over a century ago. As noted Texas author John Graves once wrote, "The Hill Country's charm is quiet, and it tends to induce a taste for quiet pleasures in those who go there."

For more information on the Hill Country, including a 264-page guide to the Lone Star State and a highway map, call the State Department of Highways and Public Transportation at (800) 8888-TEX.

FESTIVALS

JANUARY

Los Pastores. The San Antonio Conservation Society Mission hosts this Christmas miracle play at Mission San Jose every season. The play itself dates back to the days of medieval Spain. (210) 227-4262.

Miller Lite River Bottom Festival and Mud Parade. It takes a mighty festive city to turn the draining and cleaning of the river into a party, but, hey, San Antonio's just that kind of place. The Mud King and Mud Queen preside over the festivities. (210) 227-4262.

FEBRUARY

Livestock Show and Rodeo. Ready, set, rodeo! If you're looking for a taste of a traditional Texas get-together, attend this 16-day show and rodeo at the Joe and Harry Freeman Coliseum. Activities include a rodeo, a Western parade, a carnival midway, and plenty of Western fun. (210) 225-5851.

MARCH

Alamo Memorial Day. March 6 is the anniversary of the fall of the Alamo, and the event is remembered with a pre-dawn reenactment of the siege. This is the only day of the year when photography is permitted inside the Alamo. (210) 225-1391.

Newport Jazz Festival. Enjoy the sounds of jazz at this annual festival, now in its 40th year. The event is sponsored by Arts San Antonio. (210) 226-2891.

St. Patrick's Day. Grab your green and head to the river. Festivities include a downtown street parade (one of the largest in the Southwest) and the dyeing of the river green. For the day, the San Antonio River is renamed "The River Shannon," and mariachi music gives way to Irish song and dance. (210) 497-8435.

APRIL

Fiesta San Antonio. This is the granddaddy of all San Antonio celebrations, a 10-day blowout similar in scale to New Orleans's

Mardi Gras. Over 150 events take place during this mid-April party, ranging from parades to concerts to elaborate balls. Three parades bring Texas-sized crowds downtown. The Texas Cavalier's River Parade is the first, cruising the river to crowds of 175,000. Later in the week, the Battle of Flowers Parade, with brightly colored floats and the Queen of the Order of the Alamo, draws as many as 375,000 onlookers. Finally, the Fiesta Flambeau parade fills the streets with lighted floats, marching bands, and 400,000 onlookers. Another popular event is the San Antonio Conservation Society's Night in Old San Antonio, called "NIOSA" by locals. This is a foodie's paradise, too, with over 200 food booths. (210) 227-5191.

Starving Artists Show. The work of over 1,000 local artists lines the sidewalk of the River Walk and La Villita during this weekend-long show to benefit the hungry. It's held the first weekend of the month. (210) 226-3593.

Viva Botanica. Celebrate spring blossoms at the San Antonio Botanical Gardens during this colorful event. Along with 33 acres of spring flowers, the festival includes art displays, live entertainment, and food booths. (210) 821-5143.

MAY

Cinco de Mayo. This event celebrates Mexico's independence from France on the fifth of May, or "Cinco de Mayo." The city celebrates with a Cinco de Mayo Battle Ceremony at the Mexican Cultural Institute and festivities at Market Square. (210) 227-0123 or 299-8600.

Return of the Chili Queens. This is the time to indulge your taste for chili, the spicy concoction started by women known as "chili queens." To celebrate the state dish, booths are set up every Memorial Day. (210) 207-8600.

Tejano Conjunto Festival. Take the liveliness of Mexican music, mix in the accordion beat of German music, and you have *conjunto,* a unique sound born in South Texas. This festival celebrates the best of the *conjunto* musicians. (210) 271-3151.

JUNE

Fiesta Noche Del Rio. You know it's summer when Fiesta Noche Del Rio begins. The Arneson River Theatre has come alive with this summer production for nearly four decades. The show celebrates the many cultures of San Antonio through song and dance every Tuesday, Friday, and Saturday night through August. (210) 226-4651.

JULY

Contemporary Art Month. For a decade, the work of San Antonio's artists has been recognized in July with exhibits and performances. Over 70 events honor the city's performing and visual arts. (210) 224-1848.

Fiesta Noche Del Rio continues at the Arneson River Theatre. (210) 226-4651.

AUGUST

Fiesta Noche Del Rio continues at the Arneson River Theatre. (210) 226-4651.

Texas Folklife Festival. This four-day celebration in early August captures one of San Antonio's top events. Held at the Institute of Texan Cultures, the festival carries out the museum's purpose—to recognize the contributions of the many cultures that settled Texas. The festival accomplishes that goal with song, folk dance, game demonstrations, crafts exhibits and demonstrations, and lots of ethnic food. (210) 558-2300.

SEPTEMBER

Diez y Seis De Septiembre. September 16, the anniversary of Mexican independence, is celebrated with festivals at La Villita, the Arneson River Theatre, Market Square, and Guadalupe Plaza. (800) 447-3372.

El Grito (Cry for Freedom) Ceremony. On September 15, 1810, Father Hidalgo y Costilla gave the "El Grito" speech to launch Mexico's rebellion against Spain. The reenactment of "El Grito" takes place at the Plaza Mexico in HemisFair Park, followed by plenty of music and dance. (210) 227-9145.

Pachanga del Rio. This restaurant-sponsored event gives locals and vacationers the opportunity to stroll the River Walk and sample the food at 25 establishments along the way. (210) 227-4262.

OCTOBER

Day at Old Fort Sam. The historic Quadrangle at Fort Sam Houston recalls the days of Army life in frontier Texas. (210) 226-1216.

Greek Funstival. Enjoy Greek food, dances, and music at the St. Sophia Greek Orthodox Church at this fall festival, now in its fourth decade. (210) 735-5051.

International San Antonio Inter-American Bookfair and Literary Festival. The works of over 50 international publishers are honored during October with exhibits, readings, and workshops at the Guadalupe Cultural Arts Center. (210) 271-3151.

River Art Show. The River Walk is lined with the work of hundreds of Texas artists during early October. (210) 226-8752.

LATE NOVEMBER AND DECEMBER

Fiesta de las Luminarias. Thousands of *luminarias,* tiny candles in sand-weighted paper bags, guide visitors to the River Walk during this special Christmas celebration. This is one of the most beautiful Christmas displays in the nation. (210) 227-4262.

Fiestas Navideñas. Market Square takes on the holiday spirit with piñata parties, the blessing of the animals, and, of course, a visit from Pancho Claus. (210) 299-8600.

Holiday Light Magic at Sea World. A holiday show at the Sea Lion, Walrus, and Otter Stadium kicks off the holiday celebration, followed by a laser show conducted to holiday music and appearances by the Anheuser-Busch Clydesdales. A mile and a half of lighting displays continue the holiday fun. (210) 523-3611.

Holiday River Festival. The River Walk is transformed into a Christmas wonderland with the addition of 50,0000 tiny lights. On the lighting night following Thanksgiving, the river hosts a floating parade. (210) 227-4262.

Las Posadas. This beautiful ceremony dramatizes Joseph and Mary's search for an inn with costumed children leading a procession down the River Walk. Holiday songs ring out in both English and Spanish. (800) 447-3372.

A Lone Star Christmas at Fiesta Texas. The Fiesta Texas theme park is transformed into a holiday headquarters with 16 miles of Christmas lights and a 110-foot tall "Tree of Lights." Two holiday shows bring in Christmas cheer along with a five-course holiday buffet and Christmas carols. Ice skating and an appearance by Santa round out the festivities. (210) 697-5050.

O Tannenbaum German Christmas Market. The Plaza San Antonio hosts this German Christmas market. Shop for crafts while listening to German music and dining on *wienerschnitzel* or sausage. Scheduled for the weekend following Thanksgiving. (210) 229-1000.

INDEX

ABOUT THE AUTHORS

John Bigley and Paris Permenter are a husband-wife team of travel writers. Longtime residents of Central Texas, they make their home in the Hill Country west of Austin near Lake Travis.

John and Paris write frequently about Texas and other destinations for numerous magazines and newspapers. Their articles and photos have appeared in *Reader's Digest, Texas Highways, Houston Post, Austin American-Statesman, San Antonio Express-News, Denver Post, Dallas Morning News,* and many other publications. They also write a monthly column on day trip travel for San Antonio's *Fiesta* magazine.

John and Paris's other books include *Texas Barbecue* and *Day Trips From San Antonio and Austin* (now in its second edition). *Texas Barbecue,* published by Pig Out Publications of Kansas City, is a guide to the best pits, products, and prize-winning recipes in the Lone Star State and was named Best Regional Book by the Mid-America Publishers Association.

Both Paris and John are members of the American Society of Journalists and Authors. John is a member of the Outdoor Writers Association of America, and Paris is a member of the Society of American Travel Writers.

ORDER FORM

ORDER DIRECT—CALL (800) 877-3119 OR FAX (816) 531-6113

Please rush the following book(s) to me:

___ copy(s) **THE ALAMO CITY GUIDE** for $9.95

___ copy(s) **DAY TRIPS FROM SAN ANTONIO AND AUSTIN** for $11.95

___ copy(s) **DAY TRIPS FROM KANSAS CITY** for $10.95

___ copy(s) **DAY TRIPS FROM NASHVILLE** for $10.95

___ copy(s) **DALLAS CUISINE** for $14.95

___ copy(s) **SAN ANTONIO CUISINE** for $14.95

___ copy(s) **TEXAS BARBECUE** for $14.95

Shipping and handling to be added as follows:
1 book = $3.75; 2 books = $4.75; 3–5 books = $6.00

METHOD OF PAYMENT

___ Enclosed is my check for $_____ (payable to Two Lane Press, Inc.)

___ Please charge to my credit card: _____VISA _____ MasterCard

Acct. # _____ Exp. date _____

Signature _____

SHIP TO: _____ **GIFT/SHIP TO:** _____

_____ _____

_____ _____

_____ _____

_____ _____

_____ **FROM:** _____

MAIL COMPLETED ORDER FORM TO:
Two Lane Press, Inc. • 4245 Walnut Street • Kansas City, MO 64111